Matthew through Acts & Ancient Rome

Second Edition

*A Year of Lesson Plans
for History, Geography, and Bible
(Grades 1–12)*

by
Sonya Shafer

Matthew through Acts and Ancient Rome, Second Edition
© 2013, Sonya Shafer

All rights reserved. No part of this work may be reproduced or distributed in any form by any means—graphic, electronic, or mechanical, including photocopying, recording, taping, or storing in information storage and retrieval systems—without written permission from the publisher.

ISBN 978-1-61634-243-2 printed
ISBN 978-1-61634-244-9 electronic download

Cover Design: John Shafer

Published by
Simply Charlotte Mason, LLC
930 New Hope Road #11-892
Lawrenceville, Georgia 30045

SimplyCharlotteMason.com

Contents

How to Use 7
Complete Year's Book List 9

Term 1 13
    Lesson 1: (*Bible*) John the Baptist Is Born 17
    Lesson 2: (*Bible*) Jesus Is Born 18
    Lesson 3: (*Geography & History*) Visit 1 to Europe & Various Readings 18
    Lesson 4: (*History*) The First Settlers 19
    Lesson 5: (*History*) The Clever Trick 19
    Lesson 6: (*Bible*) Magi Present Gifts to Jesus 20
    Lesson 7: (*Bible*) Preparation for Ministry 20
    Lesson 8: (*Geography & History*) Visit 2 to Europe & Various Readings 21
    Lesson 9: (*History*) The Wolf and the Twins 21
    Lesson 10: (*History*) The Maidens Carried Off 21
    Lesson 11: (*Bible*) John the Baptist Announces Jesus 22
    Lesson 12: (*Bible*) Jesus Turns Water to Wine; Nicodemus 22
    Lesson 13: (*Geography & History*) Visit 3 to Europe & Various Readings 23
    Lesson 14: (*History*) Death of Romulus 23
    Lesson 15: (*History*) The Quarrel with Alba 24
    Lesson 16: (*Bible*) The Woman at the Well 24
    Lesson 17: (*Bible*) Jesus Heals the Nobleman's Son 25
    Lesson 18: (*Geography & History*) Visit 4 to Europe & Various Readings 26
    Lesson 19: (*History*) Tarquin and the Eagle 26
    Lesson 20: (*History*) The King Outwitted 27
    Lesson 21: (*Bible*) Jesus Heals the Paralytic; Rejected at Nazareth 27
    Lesson 22: (*Bible*) Jesus Continues to Heal; Calls Disciples 28
    Lesson 23: (*Geography & History*) Visit 5 to Europe & Various Readings 28
    Lesson 24: (*History*) The Ungrateful Children 29
    Lesson 25: (*History*) Tarquin's Poppies 29
    Lesson 26: (*Bible*) Sermon on the Mount, part 1 30
    Lesson 27: (*Bible*) Sermon on the Mount, part 2 30
    Lesson 28: (*Geography & History*) Visit 6 to Europe & Various Readings 30
    Lesson 29: (*History*) The Death of Lucretia 31
    Lesson 30: (*History*) A Roman Triumph 31
    Lesson 31: (*Bible*) Jesus Heals and Reassures 32
    Lesson 32: (*Bible*) Jesus Challenges Unbelief 32
    Lesson 33: (*Geography & History*) Visit 7 to Europe & Various Readings 33
    Lesson 34: (*History*) The Defense of the Bridge 33
    Lesson 35: (*History*) The Burnt Hand 33
    Lesson 36: (*Bible*) Parables; Calms the Storm 34
    Lesson 37: (*Bible*) Jesus' Power Over Demons and Death 34
    Lesson 38: (*Geography & History*) Visit 8 to Europe & Various Readings 35
    Lesson 39: (*History*) The Wrongs of the Poor 35
    Lesson 40: (*History*) The Story of Coriolanus 36
    Lesson 41: (*Bible*) Jesus Sends Out the Twelve; John Beheaded 36
    Lesson 42: (*Bible*) Jesus Feeds the Five Thousand 36
    Lesson 43: (*Geography & History*) Visit 9 to Europe & Various Readings 37
    Lesson 44: (*History*) The Farmer Hero 37
    Lesson 45: (*History*) The New Laws 38

Lesson 46: (*Bible*) Jesus Disputes the Pharisees and Heals 38
Lesson 47: (*Bible*) The Transfiguration; More Parables 39
Lesson 48: (*Geography & History*) Visit 10 to Europe & Various Readings 39
Lesson 49: (*History*) The Plans of a Traitor 40
Lesson 50: (*History*) The School-Teacher Punished 40
Lesson 51: (*Bible*) Jesus Teaches at the Feast of Tabernacles 41
Lesson 52: (*Bible*) Jesus Defends His Deity 41
Lesson 53: (*Geography & History*) Visit 11 to Europe & Various Readings 41
Lesson 54: (*History*) The Sacred Geese 42
Lesson 55: (*History*) Two Heroes of Rome 42
Lesson 56: (*Bible*) Exam or Catch Up 42
Lesson 57: (*Bible*) Exam or Catch Up 43
Lesson 58: (*Geography*) Visit 12 to Europe 44
Lesson 59: (*History*) Catch Up, Project, or Exam 44
Lesson 60: (*History*) Catch Up, Project, or Exam 44

Term 2 .... **47**

Lesson 61: (*Bible*) Jesus Heals the Blind Man 51
Lesson 62: (*Bible*) Jesus Sends Out the Seventy-Two 51
Lesson 63: (*Geography & History*) Visit 13 to Europe & Various Readings 51
Lesson 64: (*History*) The Disaster at the Caudine Forks 52
Lesson 65: (*History*) Pyrrhus and His Elephants 52
Lesson 66: (*Bible*) Jesus' Teaching on Prayer 53
Lesson 67: (*Bible*) Warnings and Encouragement 53
Lesson 68: (*Geography & History*) Visit 14 to Europe & Various Readings 53
Lesson 69: (*History*) Ancient Ships 54
Lesson 70: (*History*) Hannibal Crosses the Alps 54
Lesson 71: (*Bible*) Healing on the Sabbath 55
Lesson 72: (*Bible*) Jesus at the Pharisee's House; Parables 55
Lesson 73: (*Geography & History*) Visit 15 to Europe & Various Readings 56
Lesson 74: (*History*) The Inventor Archimedes 56
Lesson 75: (*History*) The Roman Conquests 57
Lesson 76: (*Bible*) Teachings About This Life and the Next 57
Lesson 77: (*Bible*) Jesus Raises Lazarus from the Dead 58
Lesson 78: (*Geography & History*) Visit 16 to Europe & Various Readings 58
Lesson 79: (*History*) Roman Amusements 59
Lesson 80: (*History*) The Death of Tiberius Gracchus 59
Lesson 81: (*Bible*) Ten Lepers Healed; More Parables 60
Lesson 82: (*Bible*) The Rich Young Ruler; Blind Bartimaeus 60
Lesson 83: (*Geography & History*) Visit 17 to Europe & Various Readings 60
Lesson 84: (*History*) Jugurtha, King of Numidia 61
Lesson 85: (*History*) The Social War 61
Lesson 86: (*Bible*) Zacchaeus; Jesus Anointed at Bethany 62
Lesson 87: (*Bible*) The Triumphal Entry 62
Lesson 88: (*Geography & History*) Visit 18 to Europe & Various Readings 63
Lesson 89: (*History*) The Proscription Lists 63
Lesson 90: (*History*) The Revolt of the Slaves 64
Lesson 91: (*Bible*) Parables and Teaching 64
Lesson 92: (*Bible*) Seven Woes; The Widow's Mite 65
Lesson 93: (*Geography & History*) Visit 19 to Europe & Various Readings 65
Lesson 94: (*History*) The Conspiracy of Catiline 66

Lesson 95: (*History*) Caesar's Conquests 66
Lesson 96: (*Bible*) Jesus Predicts His Death 67
Lesson 97: (*Bible*) Signs of the End of the Age 67
Lesson 98: (*Geography & History*) Visit 20 to Europe & Various Readings 68
Lesson 99: (*History*) The Battle of Pharsalia 68
Lesson 100: (*History*) The Second Triumvirate 68
Lesson 101: (*Bible*) Parables of the End of the Age 69
Lesson 102: (*Bible*) The Last Supper 69
Lesson 103: (*Geography & History*) Visit 21 to Europe & Various Readings 70
Lesson 104: (*History*) Antony and Cleopatra 70
Lesson 105: (*History*) The Augustan Age 71
Lesson 106: (*Bible*) Jesus Washes the Disciples' Feet 71
Lesson 107: (*Bible*) Jesus Comforts His Disciples 72
Lesson 108: (*Geography & History*) Visit 22 to Europe & Various Readings 72
Lesson 109: (*History*) Varus Avenged 72
Lesson 110: (*History*) Tiberius Smothered 73
Lesson 111: (*Bible*) Jesus Prays for His Disciples 74
Lesson 112: (*Bible*) Jesus Is Arrested and Tried 74
Lesson 113: (*Geography & History*) Visit 23 to Europe & Various Readings 74
Lesson 114: (*Bible*) Jesus Is Crucified 75
Lesson 115: (*Bible*) Jesus' Resurrection 75
Lesson 116: (*Bible*) Exam or Catch Up 76
Lesson 117: (*Bible*) Exam or Catch Up 76
Lesson 118: (*Geography*) Visit 24 to Europe 77
Lesson 119: (*History*) Catch Up, Project, or Exam 77
Lesson 120: (*History*) Catch Up, Project, or Exam 77

Term 3 .... **79**
Lesson 121: (*Bible*) Jesus Appears to His Disciples 83
Lesson 122: (*Bible*) Jesus Ascends to Heaven 83
Lesson 123: (*Geography & History*) Visit 25 to Europe & Various Readings 83
Lesson 124: (*History*) The Wild Caligula 84
Lesson 125: (*History*) Nero's First Crimes 84
Lesson 126: (*Bible*) Many Believe at Pentecost 85
Lesson 127: (*Bible*) Peter and John Preach 85
Lesson 128: (*Geography & History*) Visit 26 to Europe & Various Readings 86
Lesson 129: (*Bible*) Ananias and Sapphira 86
Lesson 130: (*Bible*) Stephen Is Stoned 87
Lesson 131: (*Bible*) Philip and the Ethiopian 87
Lesson 132: (*Bible*) Saul Becomes a Believer 88
Lesson 133: (*Geography & History*) Visit 27 to Europe & Various Readings 88
Lesson 134: (*Bible*) The Gospel Goes to the Gentiles 89
Lesson 135: (*Bible*) Peter's Explanation and Escape 89
Lesson 136: (*Bible*) Barnabas and Paul Start Off 90
Lesson 137: (*History*) City 91
Lesson 138: (*Geography & History*) Visit 28 to Europe & Various Readings 91
Lesson 139: (*History*) City (continued) 91
Lesson 140: (*History*) City (concluded) 92
Lesson 141: (*Bible*) Reporting on God's Work 92
Lesson 142: (*Bible*) Paul and Silas Travel 93
Lesson 143: (*Geography & History*) Visit 29 to Europe & Various Readings 93

Lesson 144: (*Bible*) The Gospel in Greece 94
Lesson 145: (*Bible*) A Riot in Ephesus 94
Lesson 146: (*Bible*) Paul's Farewell 95
Lesson 147: (*Bible*) Paul Arrested in Jerusalem 96
Lesson 148: (*Geography & History*) Visit 30 to Europe & Various Readings 96
Lesson 149: (*Bible*) Paul on Trial 97
Lesson 150: (*Bible*) Paul Appeals to Caesar Nero 97
Lesson 151: (*Bible*) Paul in Rome 98
Lesson 152: (*History*) The Christians Persecuted 98
Lesson 153: (*Geography & History*) Visit 31 to Europe & Various Readings 99
Lesson 154: (*History*) Two Short Reigns 99
Lesson 155: (*History*) The Roman Colosseum 100
Lesson 156: (*History*) The Roman Colosseum (concluded) 100
Lesson 157: (*History*) The Buried Cities 101
Lesson 158: (*Geography & History*) Visit 32 to Europe & Various Readings 101
Lesson 159: (*History*) The Emperor's Tablets 101
Lesson 160: (*History*) Polycarp 102
Lesson 161: (*History*) The Great Wall 102
Lesson 162: (*History*) The Model Pagan 103
Lesson 163: (*Geography & History*) Visit 33 to Europe & Various Readings 103
Lesson 164: (*History*) An Unnatural Son 104
Lesson 165: (*History*) Origen 104
Lesson 166: (*History*) Invasion of the Goths 105
Lesson 167: (*History*) A Prophecy Fulfilled 105
Lesson 168: (*Geography & History*) Visit 34 to Europe & Various Readings 105
Lesson 169: (*History*) Athanasius 106
Lesson 170: (*History*) The Roman Empire Divided 106
Lesson 171: (*History*) Ambrose 107
Lesson 172: (*History*) Augustine 107
Lesson 173: (*Geography & History*) Visit 35 to Europe & Various Readings 108
Lesson 174: (*History*) Jerome 108
Lesson 175: (*History*) Sieges of Rome 108
Lesson 176: (*Bible*) Exam or Catch Up 109
Lesson 177: (*Bible*) Exam or Catch Up 109
Lesson 178: (*Geography*) Visit 36 to Europe 110
Lesson 179: (*History*) Catch Up, Project, or Exam 110
Lesson 180: (*History*) Catch Up, Project, or Exam 111

Why I Wrote These Lessons 115
Charlotte Mason Methods Used in This Study 116
A Word on Mythology 118
Suggestions toward Calculating Credits 119

How to Use

This book of lesson plans contains book suggestions and assignments for every grade level, so you can combine all of your students into one family study.

- The **Family** instructions are for everyone to do together.
- Additional **Grade Level** assignments are given for students to complete either independently or with the parent. Your choice.
- **Optional** hands-on activities are also listed. Feel free to skip them, substitute different ones, or add more.

Complete one lesson per day to finish this study in a school year. The lesson plans in this book follow this five-day schedule for the first two Terms. In Term 3 the schedule will vary as Early Church history meshes with the history of Ancient Rome.

Day 1	Day 2	Day 3	Day 4	Day 5
Bible	Bible	Geography and History *(Independent reading for grades 4–12)*	History	History

You will find lots of helpful information and Internet links on the Links and Tips page for this book at http://simplycm.com/matthew-links

Complete Year's Book List

Family (all students)
- Bible
- *City: A Story of Roman Planning and Construction* by David Macaulay
    In typical Macaulay style, the story of planning and constructing a fictional Roman city is presented and detailed with lots of illustrations. Fascinating for all ages.
- *Material World* **and** *Hungry Planet: What the World Eats* by Peter Menzel
    These two wonderful living geography books are used with our *Visits to…* books every year in all the grades.
- *Peril and Peace* (History Lives series, Volume 1: Chronicles of the Ancient Church) by Mindy and Brandon Withrow
    Living stories that introduce important men in church history Not every biography in the book will be used in the plans for Family, but the additional biographies are assigned to the older students.
- *The Roman Colosseum* by Elizabeth Mann
    An interesting introduction to the Colosseum; similar in style to David Macaulay's books but not as much detail.
- *The Story of the Romans* by H. A. Guerber, edited by Christine Miller (Nothing New Press edition)
    A living narrative that weaves the story of Ancient Rome. This edited version removes evolutionary comments and honors the Biblical accounts.
- *The Stuff They Left Behind: From the Days of Ancient Rome* portfolio
    A collection of large full-color photographs of artifacts with leading thoughts and discussion questions.
- *Then and Now Bible Maps* from Rose Publishing
    An excellent geography resource used in three of our six history studies.
- *Visits to Europe* notebook by Sonya Shafer (one for each student)
    Each *Visits to…* book guides your student to spend time exploring a continent or region through map work, living books, and the personal photographs and living travelogue contained in *Material World* and *Hungry Planet: What the World Eats*. Ideas are also included for additional activities.

plus…
Grades 1–3
- *Detectives in Togas* by Henry Winterfeld (if desired)
- *Mystery of the Roman Ransom* by Henry Winterfeld (if desired)
    Students in grades 1–3 may also listen in on these Roman mysteries recommended for grades 4–6 if desired.

Grades 4–6
- *Detectives in Togas* by Henry Winterfeld
- *Mystery of the Roman Ransom* by Henry Winterfeld
    Both books by Winterfeld are fun mysteries set in Ancient Rome. Students will be introduced to daily life in that era even as they seek to solve the not-too-simple mysteries.
- *Galen and the Gateway to Medicine* by Jeanne Bendick
    A wonderful introduction to this scientist of Ancient Rome.

Grades 7–9
- *Augustus Caesar's World* by Genevieve Foster
    Though the author does a wonderful job giving a sense of all that was happening in the world during Augustus Caesar's lifetime, she does present all of the religious beliefs as equal. If your child is able to discern as he or she reads, this book should prove valuable and provide good discussion material. If your child is not as grounded in truth, you may want to use the alternate books listed next.
- OR *Beric the Briton* by G. A. Henty and *For the Temple* by G. A. Henty
    Historical fiction by a master storyteller. *Beric the Briton* focuses on life in Britain before Rome conquered it. *For the*

Temple is set in Jerusalem in A.D. 70 when Titus desecrated and destroyed the Temple.
- Book of Centuries (one for each student)
- *The Bronze Bow* by Elizabeth George Speare
    A classic historical fiction that centers around life during the time of Christ and how one boy meets Jesus.
- *Discovering Doctrine* by Sonya Shafer (one for each student)
    A multi-year project for observing, recording, and organizing Biblical truths as the student reads through the Bible.
- *Foundations in Romans: A Romans Bible Study* by Sonya Shafer (one for each student)
    Students will work their way through the book of Romans, digging deeper into word meanings and narrating every paragraph. An in-depth study of this letter Paul wrote to believers living in Ancient Rome.

Grades 10–12

- *The Apostle: A Life of Paul* by John Pollock
    A superbly-crafted, extensively-researched living narrative of the life of Paul that fills in the spaces between the glimpses of his life that we see in Acts, interweaving them with details on Jewish culture, geography, and Ancient Roman practices. Of course, some details must be speculative, but those are clearly labeled as such and do not detract from the power of this resource. What *Adam and His Kin* does for Genesis, *The Apostle* does for Acts and the epistles. (Reserved for the upper grades because of some of the descriptions of sinful cities that Paul visited and preached in. Their sinful practices are not in any way sensationalized or presented inappropriately, but they are mentioned to give a better idea of the culture in which he ministered.)
- *Augustus Caesar's World* by Genevieve Foster
    Though the author does a wonderful job giving a sense of all that was happening in the world during Augustus Caesar's lifetime, she does present all of the religious beliefs as equal. Encourage your child to discern as he or she reads; this book should prove valuable and provide good discussion material.
- *Ben-Hur* by Lew Wallace
    A classic historical fiction set in the time of Christ.
- Book of Centuries (one for each student)
- *Discovering Doctrine* by Sonya Shafer (one for each student)
    A multi-year project for observing, recording, and organizing Biblical truths as the student reads through the Bible.
- *Foundations in Romans: A Romans Bible Study* by Sonya Shafer (one for each student)
    Students will work their way through the book of Romans, digging deeper into word meanings and narrating every paragraph. An in-depth study of this letter Paul wrote to believers living in Ancient Rome.
- *Peril and Peace* (History Lives series, Volume 1: Chronicles of the Ancient Church) by Mindy and Brandon Withrow
    Living stories that introduce important men in church history. Students in grades 10–12 will read all of this book, while the Family reads selected biographies from it.
- *Plutarch's Lives*, biographies of Julius Caesar and Marc Antony, by Plutarch
    Biographies of great Romans written by a man who lived in Roman times.

Optional
- Various materials for hands-on projects

Suggestions for
Where to Find the Books

Simply Charlotte Mason
- Book of Centuries (one for each student in grades 7–12)
- *Discovering Doctrine* by Sonya Shafer (one for each student in grades 7–12)
- *Foundations in Romans: A Romans Bible Study* by Sonya Shafer (one for each student in grades 7–12)
- *The Stuff They Left Behind: From the Days of Ancient Rome* portfolio (Family)
- *Visits to Europe* notebook by Sonya Shafer (one for each student in the Family)

Public Domain
(You can probably download these for free at http://gutenberg.org, http://books.google.com, or http://archive.org.)
- *Ben-Hur* by Lew Wallace (grades 10–12)
- *Beric the Briton* by G. A. Henty (grades 7–9)
- *Plutarch's Lives*, biographies of Julius Caesar and Marc Antony, by Plutarch (grades 10–12)
- *For the Temple* by G. A. Henty (grades 7–9)

Your Local Library
(These are the titles that a library is most likely to have. You might also check for the titles listed under Your Favorite Book Store. If your library does not have access to a book listed here, add it to your Book Store list.)
- *The Bronze Bow* by Elizabeth George Speare (grades 7–9)
- *City: A Story of Roman Planning and Construction* by David Macaulay (Family)
- *Galen and the Gateway to Medicine* by Jeanne Bendick (grades 4–6)
- *The Roman Colosseum* by Elizabeth Mann (Family)

Your Favorite Book Store
(Check http://amazon.com, http://christianbook.com, http://rainbowresource.com, or other favorite book sources.)
- *The Apostle: A Life of Paul* by John Pollock (grades 10–12)
- *Augustus Caesar's World* by Genevieve Foster (grades 7–12)
- *Detectives in Togas* by Henry Winterfeld (grades 4–6 or 1–6)
- *Hungry Planet: What the World Eats* by Peter Menzel (Family)
- *Material World* by Peter Menzel (Family)
- *Mystery of the Roman Ransom* by Henry Winterfeld (grades 4–6 or 1–6)
- *Peril and Peace* (History Lives series, Volume 1: Chronicles of the Ancient Church) by Mindy and Brandon Withrow (Family and grades 10–12)
- *The Story of the Romans* by H. A. Guerber, edited by Christine Miller (Nothing New Press edition; for Family)
- *Then and Now Bible Maps* from Rose Publishing (Family)

Visit http://simplycm.com/matthew-links
for helpful links to the books.

Term 1
(12 weeks; 5 lessons/week)

Term 1 Book List
Family
- Bible
- *Material World* **and** *Hungry Planet: What the World Eats* by Peter Menzel
- *The Story of the Romans* by H. A. Guerber, edited by Christine Miller (Nothing New Press edition)
- *The Stuff They Left Behind: From the Days of Ancient Rome* portfolio
- *Then and Now Bible Maps* from Rose Publishing
- *Visits to Europe* notebook by Sonya Shafer (one for each student)

Plus . . .
Grades 1–3
- *Detectives in Togas* by Henry Winterfeld (if desired)

Grades 4–6
- *Detectives in Togas* by Henry Winterfeld

Grades 7–9
- Book of Centuries (one for each student)
- *The Bronze Bow* by Elizabeth George Speare
- *Discovering Doctrine* by Sonya Shafer (one for each student)
- *Foundations in Romans: A Romans Bible Study* by Sonya Shafer (one for each student)

Grades 10–12
- *Ben-Hur* by Lew Wallace
- Book of Centuries (one for each student)
- *Discovering Doctrine* by Sonya Shafer (one for each student)
- *Foundations in Romans: A Romans Bible Study* by Sonya Shafer (one for each student)
- *Plutarch's Lives* by Plutarch

Optional
- Various resources for hands-on projects

What You Will Cover As a Family

Bible: The Life of Christ in the Gospels, from John the Baptist's birth through Jesus' announcement at the Feast of Tabernacles

Geography: Europe, with special emphasis on Great Britain, Albania, and Bosnia

History: Ancient Rome, from its first settlers to the sacred geese that saved the Capitol from the Gauls

Term 1 At a Glance

	Family	Grades 1–3	Grades 4–6	Grades 7–9	Grades 10–12
Week 1, Lessons 1–5					
Bible	Life of Christ from the Gospels			Romans Study, lesson 1	Romans Study, lesson 1
Geography	Visits to Europe, Visit 1				
History	Story of the Romans, ch. 1–4		Detectives in Togas, ch. 1, 2		Ben-Hur, book 1, ch. 1–4; Plutarch's Caesar, 5 pages
Week 2, Lessons 6–10					
Bible	Life of Christ from the Gospels			Romans Study, lesson 1	Romans Study, lesson 1
Geography	Visits to Europe, Visit 2				
History	Story of the Romans, ch. 5–8		Detectives in Togas, ch. 3, 4	The Bronze Bow, ch. 1	Ben-Hur, book 1, ch. 5–8; Plutarch's Caesar, 5 pages
Week 3, Lessons 11–15					
Bible	Life of Christ from the Gospels			Romans Study, lesson 2	Romans Study, lesson 2
Geography	Visits to Europe, Visit 3				
History	Story of the Romans, ch. 9–12		Detectives in Togas, ch. 5, 6	The Bronze Bow, ch. 2	Ben-Hur, book 1, ch. 9–12 Plutarch's Caesar, 5 pages
Week 4, Lessons 16–20					
Bible	Life of Christ from the Gospels		Mark Study	Romans Study, lesson 2	Romans Study, lesson 2
Geography	Visits to Europe, Visit 4				
History	Story of the Romans, ch. 13–16		Detectives in Togas, ch. 7, 8	The Bronze Bow, ch. 3	Ben-Hur, book 1, ch. 13, 14 and book 2, ch. 1, 2; Plutarch's Caesar, 5 pages
Week 5, Lessons 21–25					
Bible	Life of Christ from the Gospels		Mark Study	Romans Study, lesson 3	Romans Study, lesson 3
Geography	Visits to Europe, Visit 5				
History	Story of the Romans, ch. 17–20		Detectives in Togas, ch. 9, 10	The Bronze Bow, ch. 4	Ben-Hur, book 2, ch. 3–6; Plutarch's Caesar, 5 pages
Week 6, Lessons 26–30					
Bible	Life of Christ from the Gospels		Mark Study	Romans Study, lesson 3	Romans Study, lesson 3
Geography	Visits to Europe, Visit 6				
History	Story of the Romans, ch. 21–24		Detectives in Togas, ch. 11, 12	The Bronze Bow, ch. 5	Ben-Hur, book 2, ch. 7 and book 3, ch. 1, 2; Plutarch's Caesar, 5 pages

Use this chart to see what your family and each of your students will be studying week by week during this term. You will also be able to see when each book is scheduled to be used.

	Family	Grades 1–3	Grades 4–6	Grades 7–9	Grades 10–12
Week 7, Lessons 31–35					
Bible	Life of Christ from the Gospels			Romans Study, lesson 4	Romans Study, lesson 4
Geography	Visits to Europe, Visit 7				
History	Story of the Romans, ch. 25–27		Detectives in Togas, ch. 13, 14	The Bronze Bow, ch. 6	Ben-Hur, book 3, ch. 3–6; Plutarch's Caesar, 5 pages
Week 8, Lessons 36–40					
Bible	Life of Christ from the Gospels		Mark Study	Romans Study, lesson 4	Romans Study, lesson 4
Geography	Visits to Europe, Visit 8				
History	Story of the Romans, ch. 28–30		Detectives in Togas, ch. 15, 16	The Bronze Bow, ch. 7	Ben-Hur, book 4, ch. 1–4; Plutarch's Caesar, 5 pages
Week 9, Lessons 41–45					
Bible	Life of Christ from the Gospels		Mark Study	Romans Study, lesson 5	Romans Study, lesson 5
Geography	Visits to Europe, Visit 9				
History	Story of the Romans, ch. 31–33		Detectives in Togas, ch. 17, 18	The Bronze Bow, ch. 8	Ben-Hur, book 4, ch. 5–8; Plutarch's Caesar, 5 pages
Week 10, Lessons 46–50					
Bible	Life of Christ from the Gospels		Mark Study	Romans Study, lesson 5	Romans Study, lesson 5
Geography	Visits to Europe, Visit 10				
History	Story of the Romans, ch. 34–36		Detectives in Togas, ch. 19, 20	The Bronze Bow, ch. 9	Ben-Hur, book 4, ch. 9–12; Plutarch's Caesar, 5 pages
Week 11, Lessons 51–55					
Bible	Life of Christ from the Gospels			Romans Study, Catch Up	Romans Study, Catch Up
Geography	Visits to Europe, Visit 11				
History	Story of the Romans, ch. 37, 38		Detectives in Togas, ch. 21, 22	The Bronze Bow, ch. 10	Ben-Hur, book 4, ch. 13–17; Plutarch's Caesar, finish
Week 12, Lessons 56–60					
Bible	Exam or Catch Up				
Geography	Visits to Europe, Visit 12				
History	Catch Up or Project or Exam				

Lesson 1: John the Baptist Is Born

Materials Needed
- Bible
- *Foundations in Romans* (grades 7–12)
- *Discovering Doctrine* (grades 7–12)

Family: Write on a sheet of paper or on a small white board the words "Malachi" and "Matthew," leaving a large space between them. Ask students what they know about that space between the Old Testament's events and the New Testament's events. Add any of the following points that they do not mention themselves:
- As the Old Testament closed, Judea was under the rule of Persia.
- Alexander the Great conquered Persia, and Judea came under the power of Greece (333 B.C.).
- About ten years later Alexander died, and his four generals divided his kingdom between themselves. Judea was ruled by the Egyptian division, then the Syrian division, until the Jews rose up to rebel and gained some independence (323—63 B.C.).
- Then Rome rose to power and subdued Judea again, putting various leaders in place to keep it under control (63 B.C.—the Middle Ages).

Explain that the history lessons in this study will tell the story of Ancient Rome—how it started, how it grew to be in power, and what happened to it. That story will cover hundreds of years. In the Bible lessons, you will focus on the earthly life of one Person, Jesus Christ, which took place near the middle of Rome's long history.

Remind students that the Israelites had long been watching for a Messiah, someone to save them. Discuss what they might have wanted to be saved from. Explain that the right time had come for that Messiah, and God was orchestrating the events to bring it about.

Read together Luke 1:5–80 and ask for an oral narration.

Tip: For younger children, you may want to break up the reading into two or more shorter sections and ask for a narration for each section.

Grades 7–12: Students in grades 7–12 have two ongoing Bible projects throughout this year. First, they should work their way through an inductive study of the book of Romans with *Foundations in Romans*. See the *Foundations in Romans* book for details. A pace of two weeks per lesson is outlined in these lesson plans, with extra time to catch up, if needed, at the end of each Term. Begin working on lesson 1.

Second, they should be looking for any doctrinal truths in the passages read. The Gospels and Acts contain wonderful truths that students in grades 7–12 could record in their *Discovering Doctrine* books.

Book of Centuries Timeline

TERM 1

Book of Centuries Timeline

Jesus Christ born in Bethlehem (c. 4 B.C.–0 A.D.)

Lesson 2: Jesus Is Born

Materials Needed
- Bible
- *Foundations in Romans* (grades 7–12)
- *Discovering Doctrine* (grades 7–12)

Family: Ask students what they recall from last time's reading about the events leading up to the coming of the Messiah. Read together Matthew 1:18–25 and Luke 2:1–38 and ask for an oral narration.

Tip: Each of the Gospel writers—Matthew, Mark, Luke, and John—recorded various parts of Jesus' actions and teachings. Some included details that others did not. By reading from more than one, we can gain a fuller picture of the years Jesus spent on earth.

Grades 7–12: Continue working on *Foundations in Romans*, lesson 1, and watching for truths to record in *Discovering Doctrine*.

Tip: Encourage older students to work on the Foundations in Romans *lesson each day throughout the two weeks it is mentioned, not just on the days that Bible is scheduled. A full two weeks per lesson will give them more time to concentrate and enjoy the Romans Bible study.*

Tip: Matthew 1:18-25 contains some important truths about Jesus Christ for the Discovering Doctrine *notebook.*

Lesson 3: Visit 1 to Europe & Various Readings

Materials Needed
- *Visits to Europe*
- *Detectives in Togas* (grades 4–6 or 1–6)
- *Ben-Hur* (grades 10–12)

Family: Complete Visit 1 in *Visits to Europe*.

Grades 4–6 or 1–6: Read together or assign as independent reading *Detectives in Togas*, chapter 1, "The Wrong Lantern."

Grades 10–12: Read together or assign as independent reading *Ben-Hur*, book 1, chapters 1 and 2, "Into the Desert" and "Meeting of the Wise Men."

TERM 1

Lesson 4: The First Settlers

Materials Needed
- *The Story of the Romans*
- *Ben-Hur* (grades 10–12)

Family: Display the map on page 14 in *The Story of the Romans*. Ask students to locate Italy on the map and to describe what its shape looks like to them. Read together *The Story of the Romans*, chapters 1 and 2, "The First Settlers" and "The Escape from the Burning City." Ask for an oral narration.

Tip: Narrations can be done in many ways. You may want to assign older children to do written narrations. Or visit our website at http://simplycm.com/narration-ideas for many more creative ideas that encourage students to narrate.

Grades 10–12: Read together or assign as independent reading *Ben-Hur*, book 1, chapters 3 and 4, "The Athenian Speaks—Faith" and "Speech of the Hindoo—Love."

Lesson 5: The Clever Trick

Materials Needed
- *The Story of the Romans*
- *Then and Now Bible Maps*
- *Detectives in Togas* (grades 4–6 or 1–6)
- *Plutarch's Lives* (grades 10–12)

Family: Ask students what they recall from last time's reading about Aeneas' escape from Troy. Read together *The Story of the Romans*, chapters 3 and 4, "The Clever Trick" and "The Boards are Eaten." Display map 15, in *Then and Now Bible Maps*, to trace Aeneas' route. Flip the plastic overlay, map 14, in place to see Tunis, now the capital city of Tunisia, when it is mentioned. Ask for an oral narration.

Grades 4–6 or 1–6: Read together or assign as independent reading *Detectives in Togas*, chapter 2, "A Muffled Groan."

Grades 10–12: Read together or assign as independent reading about five pages of Plutarch's biography of Caesar and ask for an oral or written narration.

Tip: Make sure older children are up to date with their Book of Centuries entries.

Book of Centuries Timeline

Aeneas escapes Troy, founds a kingdom in Italy (c. 1184 B.C.)

Book of Centuries Timeline

✝ Lesson 6: Magi Present Gifts to Jesus

Materials Needed
- Bible
- *Then and Now Bible Maps*
- *Foundations in Romans* (grades 7–12)
- *Discovering Doctrine* (grades 7–12)

Family: Ask students what they remember from last time's reading about Jesus' birth. Read together Matthew 2:1–23 and Luke 2:39–52 and ask for an oral narration.

Together locate Jerusalem and Nazareth on map 12, Holy Land - New Testament, in *Then and Now Bible Maps*. See if students can determine how far Jesus walked during his trip to the Temple. (One of the Fascinating Facts on page 10 in that book gives more details.) Draw a local comparison, if you can, to help students gain a good perspective.

Tip: Israelite men were expected to make the trip to a central location (which became the Temple at Jerusalem) three times a year to celebrate the Feasts of Passover, Shavuot (Pentecost), and Tabernacles. (See Exodus 23:14–17; 34:22–24; Deuteronomy 16:16.)

Grades 7–12: Continue working on *Foundations in Romans*, lesson 1, and watching for truths to record in *Discovering Doctrine*.

✝ Lesson 7: Preparation for Ministry

Materials Needed
- Bible
- *Foundations in Romans* (grades 7–12)
- *Discovering Doctrine* (grades 7–12)

Family: Ask students what they recall from last time's reading about Jesus' trip to the Temple at Jerusalem. Explain that the events of today's reading took place eighteen years later. Read together Mark 1:1–13 and Matthew 4:1–11 and ask for an oral narration.

Tip: These events are also recorded in Matthew 3:1–17; Luke 3:1–23; Luke 4:1–13. Assign older students to read these parallel passages if desired.

Grades 7–12: Finish *Foundations in Romans*, lesson 1, this week and keep watching for truths to record in *Discovering Doctrine*.

Tip: Mark 1:1–13 and Matthew 4:1–11 contain some truths about Jesus Christ and angels for the Discovering Doctrine *notebook.*

Lesson 8: Visit 2 to Europe & Various Readings

Materials Needed
- *Visits to Europe*
- *Material World*
- *Detectives in Togas* (grades 4–6 or 1–6)
- *The Bronze Bow* (grades 7–9)
- *Ben-Hur* (grades 10–12)

Family: Complete Visit 2 in *Visits to Europe*.

Grades 4–6 or 1–6: Read together or assign as independent reading *Detectives in Togas,* chapter 3, "A Bump of Considerable Diameter."

Grades 7–9: Read together or assign as independent reading *The Bronze Bow*, chapter 1.

Grades 10–12: Read together or assign as independent reading *Ben-Hur*, book 1, chapters 5 and 6, "The Egyptian's Story—Good Works" and "The Joppa Gate."

Lesson 9: The Wolf and the Twins

Materials Needed
- *The Story of the Romans*
- *Ben-Hur* (grades 10–12)

Family: Ask students what they recall from last time's reading about Aeneas' journeys before settling in Latium in southern Italy. Read together *The Story of the Romans*, chapters 5 and 6, "The Wolf and the Twins" and "Romulus Builds Rome." Ask for an oral narration.

Grades 10–12: Read together or assign as independent reading *Ben-Hur*, book 1, chapters 7 and 8, "Typical Characters at the Joppa Gate" and "Joseph and Mary Going to Bethlehem."

Lesson 10: The Maidens Carried Off

Materials Needed
- *The Story of the Romans*
- *Detectives in Togas* (grades 4–6 or 1–6)
- *Plutarch's Lives* (grades 10–12)

Family: Ask students what they recall from last time's reading about the

---

Book of Centuries Timeline

Romulus founds the city of Rome (753 B.C.)

Book of Centuries Timeline

Capture of the Sabine women by the Romans (730 B.C.)

twins—Romulus and Remus—and the founding of Rome. Read together *The Story of the Romans*, chapters 7 and 8, "The Maidens Carried Off" and "Union of Sabines and Romans." Ask for an oral narration.

Grades 4–6 or 1–6: Read together or assign as independent reading *Detectives in Togas,* chapter 4, "The Mathematical Burglar."

Grades 10–12: Read together or assign as independent reading about five pages of Plutarch's biography of Caesar and ask for an oral or written narration.

Tip: Make sure older children are up to date with their Book of Centuries entries.

Lesson 11: John the Baptist Announces Jesus

Materials Needed
- Bible
- *Foundations in Romans* (grades 7–12)
- *Discovering Doctrine* (grades 7–12)

Family: Discuss with students what words do and how words can affect the relationship between two people. Explain that the Apostle John described Jesus as "the Word" because He expressed God's thoughts toward man. Read together John 1:1–51 and ask for an oral narration.

Grades 7–12: Begin working on *Foundations in Romans*, lesson 2, and keep watching for truths to record in *Discovering Doctrine*.

Tip: John 1:1–51 contains some truths about Jesus Christ for the Discovering Doctrine *notebook*.

Lesson 12: Jesus Turns Water to Wine; Nicodemus

Materials Needed
- Bible
- *Then and Now Bible Maps*
- *Foundations in Romans* (grades 7–12)
- *Discovering Doctrine* (grades 7–12)

Family: Ask the students to find Cana on map 12, Holy Land - New

Testament, in *Then and Now Bible Maps*. Notice where it is in relation to Nazareth. Also point out that the region was called Galilee. If needed, compare that concept to your town that is in your county or in your state or province. Trace Jesus' journeys as you read together John 2:1—3:36, and ask for an oral narration.

Grades 7–12: Continue working on *Foundations in Romans*, lesson 2, and watching for truths to record in *Discovering Doctrine*.

Tip: John 3 contains some truths about salvation for the Discovering Doctrine *notebook.*

Lesson 13: Visit 3 to Europe & Various Readings

Materials Needed
- *Visits to Europe*
- *Detectives in Togas* (grades 4–6 or 1–6)
- *The Bronze Bow* (grades 7–9)
- *Ben-Hur* (grades 10–12)

Family: Complete Visit 3 in *Visits to Europe*.

Grades 4–6 or 1–6: Read together or assign as independent reading *Detectives in Togas*, chapter 5, "Claudia."

Grades 7–9: Read together or assign as independent reading *The Bronze Bow*, chapter 2.

Grades 10–12: Read together or assign as independent reading *Ben-Hur*, book 1, chapters 9 and 10, "The Cave at Bethlehem" and "The Light in the Sky."

Lesson 14: Death of Romulus

Materials Needed
- *The Story of the Romans*
- *Ben-Hur* (grades 10–12)

Family: Ask students what they recall from last time's reading about the Sabines and the Romans. Write these words on a sheet of paper or small white board: senators, knights, patricians, plebeians. Explain that the students will hear more about those groups of people throughout their readings on Rome. Review who each term refers to. Explain that one of the

Book of Centuries Timeline

Book of Centuries Timeline

senators played an important role in today's reading. Read together *The Story of the Romans*, chapters 9 and 10, "Death of Romulus" and "The Strange Signs of the Romans." Ask for an oral narration.

Tip: Allow the students to look at the key words you posted while they narrate. Those key words will help them stay focused and organize their thoughts. It will also be good training for them to listen for key words themselves, eventually, when none might be pointed out ahead of time.

Grades 10–12: Read together or assign as independent reading *Ben-Hur*, book 1, chapters 11 and 12, "Christ Is Born" and "The Wise Men Arrive at Jerusalem."

Lesson 15: The Quarrel with Alba

Materials Needed
- *The Story of the Romans*
- *Detectives in Togas* (grades 4–6 or 1–6)
- *Plutarch's Lives* (grades 10–12)

Family: Ask students what they recall from last time's reading about the death of Romulus and the new king of Rome, Numa Pompilius. Read together *The Story of the Romans*, chapters 11 and 12, "The Quarrel with Alba" and "The Fight between the Horatii and the Curiatii." Ask for an oral narration.

Grades 4–6 or 1–6: Read together or assign as independent reading *Detectives in Togas*, chapter 6, "Handwriting."

Grades 10–12: Read together or assign as independent reading about five pages of Plutarch's biography of Caesar and ask for an oral or written narration.

Tip: Make sure older children are up to date with their Book of Centuries entries.

The Horatii vanquish the Curiatii (670 B.C.)

Lesson 16: The Woman at the Well

Materials Needed
- Bible
- *Then and Now Bible Maps*
- *Foundations in Romans* (grades 7–12)
- *Discovering Doctrine* (grades 7–12)

Family: Ask students what they recall from last time's reading about

Jesus' discussion with Nicodemus. Remind students that Nicodemus was a Pharisee. The Pharisees were self-appointed religious leaders who felt it was their duty to make sure the Israelites obeyed God's Law. They were almost like the religious police in Israel. Read together John 4:1–3.

On map 12, Holy Land - New Testament, in *Then and Now Bible Maps*, have the students find the quickest route to go from Jerusalem to Galilee. Explain that most Jews tried to avoid the area of Samaria because they did not like the people who lived there. When Babylon conquered Judah and carried most of them away into captivity, the few who remained married non-Jewish people and settled in that area called Samaria. When the rest were released from captivity and moved back, they disdained the Samaritans. Read together John 4:4–42 and ask for an oral narration.

Tip: These events are also recorded in Mark 1:14; Luke 4:14, 15. Assign older students to read these parallel passages if desired.

Grades 4–6: Students in grades 4–6 will be reading and writing a narration for each chapter of the book of Mark during Terms 1 and 2. Assign your student to read and give a written narration of Mark 1.

Tip: If your grade 4–6 student is not yet comfortable doing oral narrations, do not assign the written narrations from Mark listed in Terms 1 and 2. If, however, your student has experience doing oral narration and is comfortable with it, now is the time to help him begin the transition to putting his thoughts on paper. Be careful not to use these written narrations as opportunities to critique. These assignments are simply exercises to begin the process of capturing his thought process in writing. Composition lessons and opportunities to fine-tune his writing style will come when he is older. Encourage his attempts and be careful not to criticize.

Grades 7–12: Continue working on *Foundations in Romans*, lesson 2, and watching for truths to record in *Discovering Doctrine*.

Tip: John 4 contains some truths about God for the Discovering Doctrine *notebook.*

✝ Lesson 17: Jesus Heals the Nobleman's Son

Materials Needed
- Bible
- *Foundations in Romans* (grades 7–12)
- *Discovering Doctrine* (grades 7–12)

Family: Ask students what they recall from last time's reading about Jesus'

Book of Centuries Timeline

trip through Samaria. Read together John 4:43–54 and ask for an oral narration.

Grades 7–12: Finish *Foundations in Romans*, lesson 2, this week and keep watching for truths to record in *Discovering Doctrine*.

Lesson 18: Visit 4 to Europe & Various Readings

Materials Needed
- *Visits to Europe*
- *Hungry Planet: What the World Eats*
- *Detectives in Togas* (grades 4–6 or 1–6)
- *The Bronze Bow* (grades 7–9)
- *Ben-Hur* (grades 10–12)

Family: Complete Visit 4 in *Visits to Europe*.

Grades 4–6 or 1–6: Read together or assign as independent reading *Detectives in Togas*, chapter 7, "The Newspaper."

Grades 7–9: Read together or assign as independent reading *The Bronze Bow*, chapter 3.

Grades 10–12: Read together or assign as independent reading *Ben-Hur*, book 1, chapters 13 and 14, "The Witnesses before Herod" and "The Wise Men Find the Child."

Lesson 19: Tarquin and the Eagle

Materials Needed
- *The Story of the Romans*
- *Ben-Hur* (grades 10–12)

Family: Ask students what they recall from last time's reading about the fight between the three Horatii and three Curiatii brothers. Discuss how the increase in people living in Rome resulted in unhealthy living conditions and the plague, which killed the king. See if students can think of any other difficulties that might appear with a rapid population increase, for Rome continued to grow. Read together *The Story of the Romans*, chapters 13 and 14, "Tarquin and the Eagle" and "The Roman Youths." Ask for an oral narration.

Grades 10–12: Read together or assign as independent reading *Ben-Hur*, book 2, chapters 1 and 2, "Jerusalem Under the Romans" and "Ben-Hur and Messala."

TERM 1

Book of Centuries Timeline

Lesson 20: The King Outwitted

Materials Needed
- *The Story of the Romans*
- *The Stuff They Left Behind: From the Days of Ancient Rome*
- *Detectives in Togas* (grades 4–6 or 1–6)
- *Plutarch's Lives* (grades 10–12)

Family: Ask students what they recall from last time's reading about how the king Ancus Martius improved Rome by building a seaport and roads. Review also the story of Tarquin and the eagle that took his cap.

Read together *The Story of the Romans*, chapters 15 and 16, "The King Outwitted" and "The Murder of Tarquin." Display and discuss the picture of the Forum from *The Stuff They Left Behind: From the Days of Ancient Rome* when you read about it in chapter 15. Ask for an oral narration at the end of the two chapters.

Grades 4–6 or 1–6: Read together or assign as independent reading *Detectives in Togas,* chapter 8, "Senator Vinicius."

Grades 10–12: Read together or assign as independent reading about five pages of Plutarch's biography of Caesar and ask for an oral or written narration.

Lesson 21: Jesus Heals the Paralytic; Rejected at Nazareth

Materials Needed
- Bible
- *Then and Now Bible Maps*
- *Foundations in Romans* (grades 7–12)
- *Discovering Doctrine* (grades 7–12)

Family: Ask students what they recall from last time's reading about Jesus' return to Galilee and the miracle that he performed there. Read together John 5:1–47 and Luke 4:14–30 and ask for an oral narration. Have the children locate on map 12, Holy Land - New Testament, in *Then and Now Bible Maps,* the regions that are mentioned in Luke 4:14–30.

Tip: John 5:1 says that Jesus went "up" to Jerusalem because it was a higher elevation, even though it was located south of Galilee.

www.SimplyCharlotteMason.com

TERM 1

Book of Centuries Timeline

Grades 7–12: Begin working on *Foundations in Romans*, lesson 3, and keep watching for truths to record in *Discovering Doctrine*.

> *Tip: John 5 contains some truths about God (the Father) and Jesus Christ (the Son) for the* Discovering Doctrine *notebook. (Note: No more tips about specific passages that contain truths for the notebooks will be listed in these lesson plans. Your students should have a pretty good grasp of what to look for by now and can continue making entries on their own.)*

Lesson 22: Jesus Continues to Heal; Calls Disciples

Materials Needed
- Bible
- *Foundations in Romans* (grades 7–12)

Family: Ask students what they recall from last time's reading about Jesus' reception in His hometown, Nazareth. Read together Luke 4:31—5:39 and ask for an oral narration.

> *Tip: These events are also recorded in Matthew 4:13–25; Mark 1:16–45; 2:1–22; Matthew 8:1–17; 9:2–17. Assign older students to read these parallel passages if desired.*

Grades 4–6: Assign your student to read and give a written narration of Mark 2.

Grades 7–12: Continue working on *Foundations in Romans*, lesson 3.

Lesson 23: Visit 5 to Europe & Various Readings

Materials Needed
- *Visits to Europe*
- *Detectives in Togas* (grades 4–6 or 1–6)
- *The Bronze Bow* (grades 7–9)
- *Ben-Hur* (grades 10–12)

Family: Complete Visit 5 in *Visits to Europe*.

Grades 4–6 or 1–6: Read together or assign as independent reading *Detectives in Togas*, chapter 9, "Wet Clothes and Empty Money-Box."

Grades 7–9: Read together or assign as independent reading *The Bronze Bow*, chapter 4.

Grades 10–12: Read together or assign as independent reading *Ben-Hur*, book 2, chapters 3 and 4, "A Judean Home" and "The Strange Things Ben-Hur Wants to Know."

Lesson 24: The Ungrateful Children

Materials Needed
- *The Story of the Romans*
- *Ben-Hur* (grades 10–12)

Family: Ask students what they recall from last time's reading about Tarquin's reign as king and his death. Read together *The Story of the Romans*, chapters 17 and 18, "The Ungrateful Children" and "The Mysterious Books." Ask for an oral narration.

Grades 10–12: Read together or assign as independent reading *Ben-Hur*, book 2, chapters 5 and 6, "Rome and Israel—A Comparison" and "The Accident to Gratus."

Lesson 25: Tarquin's Poppies

Materials Needed
- *The Story of the Romans*
- *Detectives in Togas* (grades 4–6 or 1–6)
- *Plutarch's Lives* (grades 10–12)

Family: Ask students what they recall from last time's reading about how Tullius' daughter and son-in-law usurped the throne by force. Also see if anyone can tell the story of the mysterious books. Explain that the haughty Tarquinius Superbus had a son who was just as wicked as he. Read together *The Story of the Romans*, chapters 19 and 20, "Tarquin's Poppies" and "The Oracle of Delphi." Ask for an oral narration.

Grades 4–6 or 1–6: Read together or assign as independent reading *Detectives in Togas,* chapter 10, "The Hole in the Wall."

Grades 10–12: Read together or assign as independent reading about five pages of Plutarch's biography of Caesar and ask for an oral or written narration.

Tip: Make sure older children are up to date with their Discovering Doctrine *notebooks and their Book of Centuries entries.*

TERM 1

Book of Centuries Timeline

TERM 1

Book of Centuries Timeline

Lesson 26: Sermon on the Mount, part 1

Materials Needed
- Bible
- *Foundations in Romans* (grades 7–12)

Family: Ask students what they know about the Sabbath. Read or quote together Exodus 20:8–11. Explain that the religious leaders of Jesus' day, the Pharisees, had decided to make rules that expanded on God's law for the Sabbath. They had decided just how many steps a person could walk before it was considered work. Instead of focusing on the heart and a person's attitude toward God, they started focusing on rules and regulations for a person's actions. Read together Mark 2:23—3:19 and Matthew 5:1–48 and ask for an oral narration.

Tip: These events are also recorded in Matthew 10; 12:1–21; Luke 6:1–19. Assign older students to read these parallel passages if desired.

Grades 4–6: Assign your student to read and give a written narration of Mark 3.

Grades 7–12: Continue working on *Foundations in Romans*, lesson 3.

Lesson 27: Sermon on the Mount, part 2

Materials Needed
- Bible
- *Foundations in Romans* (grades 7–12)

Family: Ask students what they recall from last time's reading about Jesus' teaching His disciples on the mountain. Explain that many people refer to this passage as the Sermon on the Mount. Today you will read the rest of it. Read together Matthew 6:1—8:1 and ask for an oral narration.

Tip: These events are also recorded in Luke 6:20–49. Assign older students to read this parallel passage if desired.

Grades 7–12: Finish *Foundations in Romans*, lesson 3, this week.

Lesson 28: Visit 6 to Europe & Various Readings

Materials Needed
- *Visits to Europe*

30   *www.SimplyCharlotteMason.com*

- *Detectives in Togas* (grades 4–6 or 1–6)
- *The Bronze Bow* (grades 7–9)
- *Ben-Hur* (grades 10–12)

Family: Complete Visit 6 in *Visits to Europe*.

Grades 4–6 or 1–6: Read together or assign as independent reading *Detectives in Togas,* chapter 11, "Snakes."

Grades 7–9: Read together or assign as independent reading *The Bronze Bow*, chapter 5.

Grades 10–12: Read together or assign as independent reading *Ben-Hur*, book 2, chapter 7, "A Galley Slave."

Lesson 29: The Death of Lucretia

Materials Needed
- *The Story of the Romans*
- *Ben-Hur* (grades 10–12)

Family: Ask students what they recall from last time's reading about Tarquin's poppies and Brutus' meeting with the oracle of Delphi. Explain that in today's reading they will hear how Brutus became the next leader of the people. Read together *The Story of the Romans*, chapters 21 and 22, "The Death of Lucretia" and "The Stern Father." Ask for an oral narration.

Grades 10–12: Read together or assign as independent reading *Ben-Hur*, book 3, chapters 1 and 2, "Quintus Arrius Goes to Sea" and "At the Oar."

Lesson 30: A Roman Triumph

Materials Needed
- *The Story of the Romans*
- *Detectives in Togas* (grades 4–6 or 1–6)
- *Plutarch's Lives* (grades 10–12)

Family: Ask students what they recall from last time's reading about how Brutus changed Rome to a republic and died defending her. Read together *The Story of the Romans*, chapters 23 and 24, "A Roman Triumph." Ask for an oral narration.

Grades 4–6 or 1–6: Read together or assign as independent reading *Detectives in Togas,* chapter 12, "A River Inside a Building?"

Grades 10–12: Read together or assign as independent reading about

Book of Centuries Timeline

Book of Centuries Timeline

five pages of Plutarch's biography of Caesar and ask for an oral or written narration.

Reminder: Bookmark or print the poem "Horatius" by Lord Thomas Babington Macaulay to read in lesson 34 if desired. You can find the poem online at http://englishverse.com.

Lesson 31: Jesus Heals and Reassures

Materials Needed
- Bible
- *Foundations in Romans* (grades 7–12)

Family: Ask students to tell what a century is. (100 years.) Explain that a centurion was an officer in the Roman army who was in charge of at least 100 soldiers. Remind students that Rome was the ruling empire at this point in Israel's history and its centurions were stationed in Judea to make sure the Israelite's obeyed Rome. Discuss what the relationship between the Israelites and the centurions may have been like. Explain that in today's reading, Jesus interacted with one of those Roman centurions. Read together Luke 7:1–50 and ask for an oral narration.

Tip: These events are also recorded in Matthew 8:5–13; 11:2–30. Assign older students to read these parallel passages if desired.

Grades 7–12: Begin working on *Foundations in Romans*, lesson 4.

Lesson 32: Jesus Challenges Unbelief

Materials Needed
- Bible
- *Foundations in Romans* (grades 7–12)

Family: Ask students what they recall from previous readings about the Pharisees' attitude toward Jesus. Explain that even when Jesus performed a miracle, as they will hear in today's reading, the Pharisees refused to believe He was sent from God. Read together Matthew 12:22–50 and ask for an oral narration.

Tip: These events are also recorded in Mark 3:20–35; Luke 8:1–3. Assign older students to read these parallel passages if desired.

Grades 7–12: Continue working on *Foundations in Romans*, lesson 4.

Lesson 33: Visit 7 to Europe & Various Readings

Materials Needed
- *Visits to Europe*
- *Detectives in Togas* (grades 4–6 or 1–6)
- *The Bronze Bow* (grades 7–9)
- *Ben-Hur* (grades 10–12)

Family: Complete Visit 7 in *Visits to Europe*.

Grades 4–6 or 1–6: Read together or assign as independent reading *Detectives in Togas,* chapter 13, "The Baths of Diana."

Grades 7–9: Read together or assign as independent reading *The Bronze Bow*, chapter 6.

Grades 10–12: Read together or assign as independent reading *Ben-Hur*, book 3, chapters 3 and 4, "Arrius and Ben-Hur on Deck" and "No. 60."

Lesson 34: The Defense of the Bridge

Materials Needed
- *The Story of the Romans*
- *Ben-Hur* (grades 10–12)

Family: Ask students what they recall from last time's reading about a Roman triumph. Read together *The Story of the Romans*, chapter 25, "The Defense of the Bridge." Ask for an oral narration.

Tip: It would make a lovely addition to this lesson to read the poem Lord Thomas Babington Macaulay wrote about Horatius and this battle. You can find the poem "Horatius" online at http://englishverse.com.

Grades 10–12: Read together or assign as independent reading *Ben-Hur*, book 3, chapters 5 and 6, "The Sea Fight" and "Arrius Adopts Ben-Hur."

Lesson 35: The Burnt Hand

Materials Needed
- *The Story of the Romans*
- *Detectives in Togas* (grades 4–6 or 1–6)
- *Plutarch's Lives* (grades 10–12)

Family: Ask students what they recall from last time's reading about Horatius and the bridge. Read together *The Story of the Romans*, chapters 26

Book of Centuries Timeline

Horatius defends the bridge over the Tiber (509—499 B.C.)

Book of Centuries Timeline

and 27, "The Burnt Hand" and "The Twin Gods." Ask for an oral narration.

Grades 4–6 or 1–6: Read together or assign as independent reading *Detectives in Togas,* chapter 14, "A Letter to the Emperor."

Grades 10–12: Read together or assign as independent reading about five pages of Plutarch's biography of Caesar and ask for an oral or written narration.

Tip: Make sure older children are up to date with their Discovering Doctrine *notebooks and their Book of Centuries entries.*

Lesson 36: Parables; Calms the Storm

Materials Needed
- Bible
- *Foundations in Romans* (grades 7–12)

Family: Ask students if they know what a parable is. If needed, explain that a parable is an earthly story that illustrates a Heavenly truth. Inform students that Jesus told many parables, and today you will read some of them. Read together Mark 4 and ask for an oral narration. Encourage students to give the main truth from each parable Jesus told.

Tip: These events are also recorded in Luke 8:4–25; Matthew 13; 8:18–27. Assign older students to read these parallel passages if desired.

Grades 4–6: Assign a written narration of Mark 4.

Grades 7–12: Continue working on *Foundations in Romans*, lesson 4.

Lesson 37: Jesus' Power Over Demons and Death

Materials Needed
- Bible
- *Then and Now Bible Maps*
- *Foundations in Romans* (grades 7–12)

Family: Ask students what they recall from last time's reading about the boat ride Jesus and His disciples had. On map 12, Holy Land - New Testament, in *Then and Now Bible Maps*, locate the Sea of Galilee and the area near the town of Gadara. Read together Mark 5:1—6:6 and ask for an oral narration.

Tip: These events are also recorded in Matthew 8:28–34; 9:1–34; Luke 8:26–56. Assign older students to read these parallel passages if desired.

Grades 4–6: Assign a written narration of Mark 5.

Grades 7–12: Finish *Foundations in Romans*, lesson 4, this week.

Lesson 38: Visit 8 to Europe & Various Readings

Materials Needed
- *Visits to Europe*
- *Detectives in Togas* (grades 4–6 or 1–6)
- *The Bronze Bow* (grades 7–9)
- *Ben-Hur* (grades 10–12)

Family: Complete Visit 8 in *Visits to Europe*.

Grades 4–6 or 1–6: Read together or assign as independent reading *Detectives in Togas,* chapter 15, "Xantippus Finds the Point."

Grades 7–9: Read together or assign as independent reading *The Bronze Bow*, chapter 7.

Grades 10–12: Read together or assign as independent reading *Ben-Hur*, book 4, chapters 1 and 2, "Ben-Hur Returns East" and "On the Orontes."

Lesson 39: The Wrongs of the Poor

Materials Needed
- *The Story of the Romans*
- *Ben-Hur* (grades 10–12)

Family: Ask students what they recall from last time's reading about Tarquin's third attempt to recover the throne in Rome. Read together *The Story of the Romans*, chapters 28 and 29, "The Wrongs of the Poor" and "The Fable of the Stomach." Ask for an oral narration.

Grades 10–12: Read together or assign as independent reading *Ben-Hur*, book 4, chapters 3 and 4, "The Demand of Simonides" and "Simonides and Esther."

Book of Centuries Timeline

TERM 1

Book of Centuries Timeline

Lesson 40: The Story of Coriolanus

Materials Needed
- *The Story of the Romans*
- *Detectives in Togas* (grades 4–6 or 1–6)
- *Plutarch's Lives* (grades 10–12)

Family: Ask students what they recall from last time's reading about the plebeians' plight and what came of it. Read together *The Story of the Romans*, chapter 30, "The Story of Coriolanus." Ask for an oral narration.

Grades 4–6 or 1–6: Read together or assign as independent reading *Detectives in Togas,* chapter 16, "Cheap Soap, Burned Oil, and Onions."

Grades 10–12: Read together or assign as independent reading about five pages of Plutarch's biography of Caesar and ask for an oral or written narration.

Lesson 41: Jesus Sends Out the Twelve; John Beheaded

Materials Needed
- Bible
- *Foundations in Romans* (grades 7–12)

Family: Ask students what they recall from last time's reading about Jesus' reception in His hometown. Read together Matthew 10:1—11:1 and Matthew 14:1–12 and ask for an oral narration.

Tip: These events are also recorded in Mark 6:7–29; Luke 9:1–9. Assign older students to read these parallel passages if desired.

Grades 7–12: Begin working on *Foundations in Romans*, lesson 5.

Lesson 42: Jesus Feeds the Five Thousand

Materials Needed
- Bible
- *Foundations in Romans* (grades 7–12)

Family: Ask students what they recall about the disciples and John the

Baptist from last time's reading. Read together John 6:1–71 and ask for an oral narration.

> *Tip: These events are also recorded in Matthew 14:13–33; Mark 6:30–56; Luke 9:10–17. Assign older students to read these parallel passages if desired.*

Grades 4–6: Assign your student to read and give a written narration of Mark 6.

Grades 7–12: Continue working on *Foundations In Romans*, lesson 5.

Lesson 43: Visit 9 to Europe & Various Readings

Materials Needed
- *Visits to Europe*
- *Material World*
- *Detectives in Togas* (grades 4–6 or 1–6)
- *The Bronze Bow* (grades 7–9)
- *Ben-Hur* (grades 10–12)

Family: Complete Visit 9 in *Visits to Europe*.

Grades 4–6 or 1–6: Read together or assign as independent reading *Detectives in Togas,* chapter 17, "A Certain Guest."

Grades 7–9: Read together or assign as independent reading *The Bronze Bow*, chapter 8.

Grades 10–12: Read together or assign as independent reading *Ben-Hur*, book 4, chapters 5 and 6, "The Grove of Daphne" and "The Mulberries of Daphne."

Lesson 44: The Farmer Hero

Materials Needed
- *The Story of the Romans*
- *Ben-Hur* (grades 10–12)

Family: Ask students what they recall from last time's reading about Coriolanus, his treatment of the plebeians, and his mother's plea. Read together *The Story of the Romans*, chapter 31, "The Farmer Hero." Ask for an oral narration.

Book of Centuries Timeline

Cincinnatus serves as dictator for 17 days (460 B.C.)

Book of Centuries Timeline

Grades 10–12: Read together or assign as independent reading *Ben-Hur*, book 4, chapters 7 and 8, "The Stadium in the Grove" and "The Fountain of Castalia."

Lesson 45: The New Laws

Materials Needed
- *The Story of the Romans*
- *Detectives in Togas* (grades 4–6 or 1–6)
- *Plutarch's Lives* (grades 10–12)

Family: Ask students what they recall from last time's reading about the farmer hero, Cincinnatus. Read together *The Story of the Romans*, chapters 32 and 33, "The New Laws" and "The Death of Virginia." Ask for an oral narration.

Grades 4–6 or 1–6: Read together or assign as independent reading *Detectives in Togas,* chapter 18, "A Banquet."

Grades 10–12: Read together or assign as independent reading about five pages of Plutarch's biography of Caesar and ask for an oral or written narration.

Tip: Make sure older children are up to date with their *Discovering Doctrine notebooks* and their Book of Centuries entries.

Lesson 46: Jesus Disputes the Pharisees and Heals

Materials Needed
- Bible
- *Then and Now Bible Maps*
- *Foundations in Romans* (grades 7–12)

Family: Ask the students what they recall from last time's reading about Jesus' miracles and many of His disciples' reaction. Review the self-appointed place of the Pharisees and explain that in today's reading they once again challenged Jesus because He didn't follow their man-made rules. Read together Mark 7:1—8:38 and use map 12, Holy Land - New Testament, in *Then and Now Bible Maps,* to trace Jesus' movements, then ask for an oral narration.

Tip: These events are also recorded in Matthew 14:34—16:28; Luke 9:18–27. Assign older students to read these parallel passages if desired.

Grades 4–6: Assign a written narration of Mark 7 and 8.

Grades 7–12: Continue working on *Foundations in Romans*, lesson 5.

Lesson 47: The Transfiguration; More Parables

Materials Needed
- Bible
- *Foundations in Romans* (grades 7–12)

Family: Ask students what they recall from last time's reading about Peter's confession of Who Jesus is. Write the word "transfigured" on a small white board or a sheet of paper. Help students define it by identifying *trans* as "change" and pointing out the word *figure*. Explain that some of the disciples saw Jesus transfigured. Read together Matthew 17:1—18:35 and ask for an oral narration.

Tip: These events are also recorded in Mark 9:1–50; Luke 9:28–50. Assign older students to read these parallel passages if desired.

Grades 4–6: Assign your student to read and give a written narration of Mark 9.

Grades 7–12: Finish *Foundations in Romans*, lesson 5, this week.

Lesson 48: Visit 10 to Europe & Various Readings

Materials Needed
- *Visits to Europe*
- *Detectives in Togas* (grades 4–6 or 1–6)
- *The Bronze Bow* (grades 7–9)
- *Ben-Hur* (grades 10–12)

Family: Complete Visit 10 in *Visits to Europe*.

Grades 4–6 or 1–6: Read together or assign as independent reading *Detectives in Togas,* chapter 19, "The Bakery."

Grades 7–9: Read together or assign as independent reading *The Bronze Bow*, chapter 9.

Book of Centuries Timeline

Book of Centuries Timeline

Grades 10–12: Read together or assign as independent reading *Ben-Hur*, book 4, chapters 9 and 10, "The Chariot Race Discussed" and "Ben-Hur Hears of Christ."

Lesson 49: The Plans of a Traitor

Materials Needed
- *The Story of the Romans*
- *Ben-Hur* (grades 10–12)

Family: Ask students what they recall from last time's reading about the new laws and the death of Virginia. Read together *The Story of the Romans*, chapter 34, "The Plans of a Traitor." Ask for an oral narration.

Grades 10–12: Read together or assign as independent reading *Ben-Hur*, book 4, chapters 11 and 12, "The Wise Servant and His Daughter" and "A Roman Orgie."

Reminder: If you want to do an optional hands-on project for lesson 59 or 60, start collecting the materials you will need.

Reminder: Start gathering the resources you will need for Term 2. See page 47.

Lesson 50: The School-Teacher Punished

Materials Needed
- *The Story of the Romans*
- *Detectives in Togas* (grades 4–6 or 1–6)
- *Plutarch's Lives* (grades 10–12)

Family: Ask students what they recall from last time's reading about the continuing conflict between patricians and plebeians and how Spurius Maelius tried to take advantage of it. Read together *The Story of the Romans*, chapters 35 and 36, "The School-Teacher Punished" and "The Invasion of the Gauls." Ask for an oral narration.

Grades 4–6 or 1–6: Read together or assign as independent reading *Detectives in Togas,* chapter 20, "Surprises."

Grades 10–12: Read together or assign as independent reading about five pages of Plutarch's biography of Caesar and ask for an oral or written narration.

Lesson 51: Jesus Teaches at the Feast of Tabernacles

Materials Needed
- Bible
- *Foundations in Romans* (grades 7–12)

Family: Explain that one of the three special feasts had come and everyone was making the trip to Jerusalem to celebrate it, the Feast of Tabernacles. But Jesus had to be careful about going. Read together John 7:1–53 and ask for an oral narration.

Grades 7–12: Use this week to catch up on *Foundations in Romans*, lessons 1–5, if needed.

Lesson 52: Jesus Defends His Deity

Materials Needed
- Bible
- *Foundations in Romans* (grades 7–12)

Family: Ask students what they recall from last time's reading about Jesus' appearance at the Feast of Tabernacles. Read together John 8:1–59 and ask for an oral narration.

Grades 7–12: Use this week to catch up on *Foundations in Romans*, lessons 1–5, if needed.

Lesson 53: Visit 11 to Europe & Various Readings

Materials Needed
- *Visits to Europe*
- *Material World*
- *Detectives in Togas* (grades 4–6 or 1–6)
- *The Bronze Bow* (grades 7–9)
- *Ben-Hur* (grades 10–12)

Family: Complete Visit 11 in *Visits to Europe*.

Grades 4–6 or 1–6: Read together or assign as independent reading *Detectives in Togas*, chapter 21, "Light."

Grades 7–9: Read together or assign as independent reading *The Bronze Bow*, chapter 10.

TERM 1

Book of Centuries Timeline

Grades 10–12: Read together or assign as independent reading *Ben-Hur*, book 4, chapters 13 and 14, "A Driver for Ilderim's Arabs" and "The Dowar in the Orchard of Palms."

Lesson 54: The Sacred Geese

Materials Needed
- *The Story of the Romans*
- *Ben-Hur* (grades 10–12)

Family: Ask students what they recall from last time's reading about the dishonest schoolmaster and the invasion of the Gauls. Read together *The Story of the Romans*, chapter 37, "The Sacred Geese." Ask for an oral narration.

Grades 10–12: Read together or assign as independent reading *Ben-Hur*, book 4, chapters 15–17, "Balthasar Impresses Ben-Hur," "Christ is Coming—Balthasar," and "The Kingdom—Spiritual or Political?"

The Gauls burn Rome (390 B.C.)

Rome rebuilt (389 B.C.)

Lesson 55: Two Heroes of Rome

Materials Needed
- *The Story of the Romans*
- *Detectives in Togas* (grades 4–6 or 1–6)
- *Plutarch's Lives* (grades 10–12)

Family: Ask students what they recall from last time's reading about the sacred geese and the assault of the Gauls. Read together *The Story of the Romans*, chapter 38, "Two Heroes of Rome." Ask for an oral narration.

Grades 4–6 or 1–6: Read together or assign as independent reading *Detectives in Togas*, chapter 22, "The Banks of the Rhine."

Grades 10–12: Read together or assign as independent reading the rest of Plutarch's biography of Caesar and ask for an oral or written narration.

Tip: Make sure older children are up to date with their Discovering Doctrine *notebooks and their Book of Centuries entries.*

Lesson 56: Bible Exam or Catch Up

Materials Needed
- Bible (if doing catch-up reading)

TERM 1

Book of Centuries Timeline

Family: Use this day to catch up on any Bible reading you need to finish, or use the questions below for the students' exam on the Life of Christ studied so far.

Tip: Exams in a Charlotte Mason school require no "cramming" or preparation. You may be pleasantly surprised at what your students remember with no prompting.

Grades 1–3: Tell an account of Jesus' healing someone.
Grades 4–6: Tell an account of a miracle Jesus performed.
Grades 7–9: "God so loved the world that He gave His only begotten Son." Tell all you can remember about Who said this to whom and the circumstances surrounding it.
Grades 10–12: Tell in full about Jesus' twelve disciples: their callings, their faith or lack of it, their questions.

Tip: You may want to assign the older students to write their exam answers. Younger students may do oral exams; you might want to write or type their answers as they tell what they know. Or, if you have students in more than one grade level, you might allow them to do their exams orally in a group. That way the older can hear the younger, and the younger can hear the older.

Lesson 57: Bible Exam or Catch Up

Materials Needed
- Bible (if doing catch-up reading)
- *Foundations in Romans*, if needed (grades 7–12)

Family: Use this day to catch up on any Bible reading you need to finish, or use the questions below for the students' exam on the Life of Christ studied so far.
Grades 1–3: Tell one of the parables that Jesus told.
Grades 4–6: Tell all you can about the relationship between the religious leaders (Pharisees) and Jesus.
Grades 7–9: Tell about a time when someone tried to stump Jesus with a tricky question. Recall all you can remember about the situation and Jesus' answer.
Grades 10–12: How did Jesus prove His deity and authority? Cite as many proofs, with their circumstances, as you can remember.

Grades 7–12: Select a chapter from Romans 1–5 and ask for a narration. Allow the student to look at the chapter outline in *Foundations in Romans* if necessary.

Book of Centuries Timeline

Lesson 58: Visit 12 to Europe

Materials Needed
- *Visits to Europe*

Family: Family: Complete Visit 12 in *Visits to Europe*.

Lesson 59: Ancient Rome Catch Up, Project, or Exam

Materials Needed
- *The Story of the Romans,* if needed
- (optional) Materials for hands-on project

Family: Use this day to catch up on any history reading you need to finish, or use the questions below for the students' exam on their Ancient Rome readings. You may also use this lesson and the next to do an optional hands-on project if you would prefer.
Grades 1–3: Tell a story of bravery in Ancient Rome.
Grades 4–6: Tell the story of Mucius the Left-Handed.
Grades 7–9: Define these English words that come from Ancient Rome and tell their background stories: *senator* and *veto*.
Grades 10–12: Describe the relationship between patricians and plebeians in Ancient Rome: who belonged to each class, what each class was afforded for rights and privileges, what struggles ensued, and what steps were taken to resolve those issues.

Optional Hands-On Project: Select a hands-on project from the Links and Tips page at http://simplycm.com/matthew-links.

Lesson 60: Ancient Rome Catch Up, Project, or Exam

Materials Needed
- *The Story of the Romans,* if needed
- (optional) Materials for hands-on project

Family: Use this day to catch up on any reading you need to finish, or use the questions below for the students' exam on their Ancient Rome readings. You may also do an optional hands-on project.
Grades 1–3: Tell the story of how geese saved the Capitol.
Grades 4–6: Tell the story of Horatius and the Bridge.
Grades 7–9: "The earth is the true mother of us all." Give the story of that remark and tell about the man who made it.

Grades 10–12: From your readings in Plutarch, describe Julius Caesar's character and cite examples to support your statements. Why is he considered such a prominent person in Roman history?

Optional Hands-On Project: Continue your selected hands-on project or start a new one if desired.

Book of Centuries Timeline

Term 2
(12 weeks; 5 lessons/week)

Term 2 Book List
Family
- Bible
- *Material World* **and** *Hungry Planet: What the World Eats* by Peter Menzel
- *The Story of the Romans* by H. A. Guerber, edited by Christine Miller (Nothing New Press edition)
- *The Stuff They Left Behind: From the Days of Ancient Rome* portfolio
- *Then and Now Bible Maps* from Rose Publishing
- *Visits to Europe* notebook (one for each student)

Plus . . .
Grades 1–3
- *Mystery of the Roman Ransom* by Henry Winterfeld (if desired)

Grades 4–6
- *Mystery of the Roman Ransom* by Henry Winterfeld

Grades 7–9
- *Augustus Caesar's World* by Genevieve Foster OR *Beric the Briton* by G. A. Henty
- Book of Centuries (one for each student)
- *The Bronze Bow* by Elizabeth George Speare
- *Discovering Doctrine* by Sonya Shafer (one for each student)
- *Foundations in Romans: A Romans Bible Study* by Sonya Shafer (one for each student)

Grades 10–12
- *Ben-Hur* by Lew Wallace
- Book of Centuries (one for each student)
- *Discovering Doctrine* by Sonya Shafer (one for each student)
- *Foundations in Romans: A Romans Bible Study* by Sonya Shafer (one for each student)
- *Plutarch's Lives* by Plutarch

Optional
- Various resources for hands-on projects

What You Will Cover As a Family

Bible: The Life of Christ in the Gospels, from Jesus' healing the blind man to Jesus' death and resurrection

Geography: Europe, with special emphasis on France, Spain, and Italy

History: Ancient Rome, from the battles with Pyrrhus to Emperor Tiberius

Term 2 At a Glance

	Family	Grades 1–3	Grades 4–6	Grades 7–9	Grades 10–12
Week 1, Lessons 61–65					
Bible	Life of Christ from the Gospels			Romans Study, lesson 6	Romans Study, lesson 6
Geography	Visits to Europe, Visit 13				
History	The Story of the Romans, ch. 39–41		Mystery of the Roman Ransom, ch. 1, 2	Bronze Bow, ch. 11; Augustus Caesar's World OR Beric the Briton, ch. 1, 2	Ben-Hur, book 5, ch. 1–4; Plutarch's Antony, 6 pages
Week 2, Lessons 66–70					
Bible	Life of Christ from the Gospels			Romans Study, lesson 6	Romans Study, lesson 6
Geography	Visits to Europe, Visit 14				
History	The Story of the Romans, ch. 42–45		Mystery of the Roman Ransom, ch. 3, 4	Bronze Bow, ch. 12; Augustus Caesar's World OR Beric the Briton, ch. 3, 4	Ben-Hur, book 5, ch. 5–8; Plutarch's Antony, 6 pages
Week 3, Lessons 71–75					
Bible	Life of Christ from the Gospels			Romans Study, lesson 7	Romans Study, lesson 7
Geography	Visits to Europe, Visit 15				
History	The Story of the Romans, ch. 46–48		Mystery of the Roman Ransom, ch. 5, 6	Bronze Bow, ch. 13; Augustus Caesar's World OR Beric the Briton, ch. 5, 6	Ben-Hur, book 5, ch. 9–12; Plutarch's Antony, 6 pages
Week 4, Lessons 76–80					
Bible	Life of Christ from the Gospels			Romans Study, lesson 7	Romans Study, lesson 7
Geography	Visits to Europe, Visit 16				
History	The Story of the Romans, ch. 49–52		Mystery of the Roman Ransom, ch. 7, 8	Bronze Bow, ch. 14; Augustus Caesar's World OR Beric the Briton, ch. 7, 8	Ben-Hur, book 5, ch. 13–16; Plutarch's Antony, 6 pages
Week 5, Lessons 81–85					
Bible	Life of Christ from the Gospels		Mark Study	Romans Study, lesson 8	Romans Study, lesson 8
Geography	Visits to Europe, Visit 17				
History	The Story of the Romans, ch. 53–56		Mystery of the Roman Ransom, ch. 9, 10	Bronze Bow, ch. 15; Augustus Caesar's World OR Beric the Briton, ch. 9, 10	Ben-Hur, book 6, ch. 1–4; Plutarch's Antony, 6 pages
Week 6, Lessons 86–90					
Bible	Life of Christ from the Gospels		Mark Study	Romans Study, lesson 8	Romans Study, lesson 8
Geography	Visits to Europe, Visit 18				
History	The Story of the Romans, ch. 57–60		Mystery of the Roman Ransom, ch. 11, 12	Bronze Bow, ch. 16; Augustus Caesar's World OR Beric the Briton, ch. 11, 12	Ben-Hur, book 6, ch. 5, 6 and book 7, ch. 1, 2; Plutarch's Antony, 6 pages

Use this chart to see what your family and each of your students will be studying week by week during this term. You will also be able to see when each book is scheduled to be used.

	Family	Grades 1–3	Grades 4–6	Grades 7–9	Grades 10–12
			Week 7, Lessons 91–95		
Bible	Life of Christ from the Gospels		Mark Study	Romans Study, lesson 9	Romans Study, lesson 9
Geography	Visits to Europe, Visit 19				
History	The Story of the Romans, ch. 61–63		Mystery of the Roman Ransom, ch. 13, 14	Bronze Bow, ch. 17; Augustus Caesar's World OR Beric the Briton, ch. 13, 14	Ben-Hur, book 7, ch. 3–5; Plutarch's Antony, 6 pages
			Week 8, Lessons 96–100		
Bible	Life of Christ from the Gospels		Mark Study	Romans Study, lesson 9	Romans Study, lesson 9
Geography	Visits to Europe, Visit 20				
History	The Story of the Romans, ch. 64–67		Mystery of the Roman Ransom, ch. 15, 16	Bronze Bow, ch. 18; Augustus Caesar's World OR Beric the Briton, ch. 15, 16	Ben-Hur, book 8, ch. 1–4; Plutarch's Antony, 6 pages
			Week 9, Lessons 101–105		
Bible	Life of Christ from the Gospels			Romans Study, lesson 10	Romans Study, lesson 10
Geography	Visits to Europe, Visit 21				
History	The Story of the Romans, ch. 68–71		Mystery of the Roman Ransom, ch. 17, 18	Bronze Bow, ch. 19; Augustus Caesar's World OR Beric the Briton, ch. 17, 18	Ben-Hur, book 8, ch. 5, 6; Plutarch's Antony, 6 pages
			Week 10, Lessons 106–110		
Bible	Life of Christ from the Gospels		Mark Study	Romans Study, lesson 10	Romans Study, lesson 10
Geography	Visits to Europe, Visit 22				
History	The Story of the Romans, ch. 72–74		Mystery of the Roman Ransom, ch. 19, 20	Bronze Bow, ch. 20; Augustus Caesar's World OR Beric the Briton, ch. 19, 20	Ben-Hur, book 8, ch. 7, 8; Plutarch's Antony, 6 pages
			Week 11, Lessons 111–115		
Bible	Life of Christ from the Gospels			Romans Study, lesson 11	Romans Study, lesson 11
Geography	Visits to Europe, Visit 23				
History			Mystery of the Roman Ransom, ch. 21, 22	Bronze Bow, ch. 21; Augustus Caesar's World OR Beric the Briton, ch. 21	Ben-Hur, book 8, ch. 9, 10; Plutarch's Antony, finish
			Week 12, Lessons 116–120		
Bible	Exam or Catch Up			Romans Study, lesson 11	Romans Study, lesson 11
Geography	Visits to Europe, Visit 24				
History	Catch Up or Project or Exam				

Lesson 61: Jesus Heals the Blind Man

Materials Needed
- Bible
- *Foundations in Romans* (grades 7–12)

Family: Ask students what they recall about Jesus' healing people. What kinds of reactions did those watching have? Explain that in today's reading, Jesus' healing ministry created a stir. Read together John 9:1—10:21 and ask for an oral narration.

Grades 7–12: Begin working on *Foundations in Romans*, lesson 6.

Lesson 62: Jesus Sends Out the Seventy-Two

Materials Needed
- Bible
- *Foundations in Romans* (grades 7–12)

Family: Ask the students what they recall from last time's reading about the stir that the healing of the blind man created. Explain that the time was drawing near for Jesus to die on the cross, and He knew it. Read together Luke 9:51—10:42 and ask for an oral narration.

Grades 7–12: Continue working on *Foundations in Romans*, lesson 6.

Lesson 63: Visit 13 to Europe & Various Readings

Materials Needed
- *Visits to Europe*
- *Hungry Planet: What the World Eats*
- *Mystery of the Roman Ransom* (grades 4–6 or 1–6)
- *The Bronze Bow* (grades 7–9)
- *Ben-Hur* (grades 10–12)

Family: Complete Visit 13 in *Visits to Europe*.

Grades 4–6 or 1–6: Read together or assign as independent reading *Mystery of the Roman Ransom*, chapter 1, "Xantippus Can't Use a Lion Either."

Grades 7–9: Read together or assign as independent reading *The Bronze Bow*, chapter 11.

Book of Centuries Timeline

www.SimplyCharlotteMason.com

Book of Centuries Timeline

Grades 10–12: Read together or assign as independent reading *Ben-Hur*, book 5, chapters 1 and 2, "Messala Doffs his Chaplet" and "Ilderim's Arabs under the Yoke."

Lesson 64: The Disaster at the Caudine Forks

Materials Needed
- *The Story of the Romans*
- *Augustus Caesar's World* OR *Beric the Briton* (grades 7–9)
- *Ben-Hur* (grades 10–12)

Family: Ask students what they recall from last time's reading about the two hero tales of Curtius and the Chasm and Valerius and the Gigantic Gaul. Read together *The Story of the Romans*, chapter 39, "The Disaster at the Caudine Forks." Ask for an oral narration.

Grades 7–9: Read together or assign as independent reading *Augustus Caesar's World*, pages xi–xiii, "Introduction," OR *Beric the Briton*, chapter 1, "A Hostage," and ask for an oral or written narration.

Grades 10–12: Read together or assign as independent reading *Ben-Hur*, book 5, chapters 3 and 4, "The Arts of Cleopatra" and "Messala on Guard."

The Appian Way constructed (312 B.C.)

Lesson 65: Pyrrhus and His Elephants

Materials Needed
- *The Story of the Romans*
- *Mystery of the Roman Ransom* (grades 4–6 or 1–6)
- *Augustus Caesar's World* OR *Beric the Briton* (grades 7–9)
- *Plutarch's Lives* (grades 10–12)

Family: Ask students what they recall from last time's reading about the examples of Roman courage and discipline on the battlefield. Read together *The Story of the Romans*, chapters 40 and 41, "Pyrrhus and His Elephants" and "The Elephants Routed." Ask for an oral narration.

Grades 4–6 or 1–6: Read together or assign as independent reading *Mystery of the Roman Ransom*, chapter 2, "Why Did the Slave Dealer Run Away?"

Grades 7–9: Read together or assign as independent reading *Augustus Caesar's World*, pages 5–13, "Under a Lucky Star" and "The Ides of March," OR *Beric the Briton*, chapter 2, "City and Forest," and ask for an oral or written narration.

Grades 10–12: Read together or assign as independent reading about six pages of Plutarch's biography of Antony and ask for an oral or written narration.

Tip: Make sure older children are up to date with their Discovering Doctrine *notebooks and their Book of Centuries entries.*

Lesson 66: Jesus' Teaching on Prayer

Materials Needed
- Bible
- *Foundations in Romans* (grades 7–12)

Family: Ask students what they recall from last time's reading about Jesus' actions in the face of His upcoming crucifixion and about His time at Mary and Martha's house. Read together Luke 11:1–54 and ask for an oral narration.

Grades 7–12: Continue working on *Foundations in Romans*, lesson 6.

Lesson 67: Warnings and Encouragement

Materials Needed
- Bible
- *Foundations in Romans* (grades 7–12)

Family: Ask students what they remember from last time's reading about Jesus' reproofs to the Pharisees. Explain that He warned His disciples about the Pharisees too. Read together Luke 12:1–59 and ask for an oral narration.

Grades 7–12: Finish *Foundations in Romans*, lesson 6, this week.

Lesson 68: Visit 14 to Europe & Various Readings

Materials Needed
- *Visits to Europe*
- *Mystery of the Roman Ransom* (grades 4–6 or 1–6)
- *The Bronze Bow* (grades 7–9)
- *Ben-Hur* (grades 10–12)

Family: Complete Visit 14 in *Visits to Europe*.

Book of Centuries Timeline

Book of Centuries Timeline

Grades 4–6 or 1–6: Read together or assign as independent reading *Mystery of the Roman Ransom*, chapter 3, "The Fearsome Ex-Gladiator."

Grades 7–9: Read together or assign as independent reading *The Bronze Bow*, chapter 12.

Grades 10–12: Read together or assign as independent reading *Ben-Hur*, book 5, chapters 5 and 6, "Ilderim and Ben-Hur Deliberate" and "Training the Four."

Lesson 69: Ancient Ships

Materials Needed
- *The Story of the Romans*
- *Augustus Caesar's World* OR *Beric the Briton* (grades 7–9)
- *Ben-Hur* (grades 10–12)

Family: Ask students what they recall from last time's reading about Pyrrhus and his elephants. Remind students, if they do not mention it, about the statement Pyrrhus made upon leaving Italy: "What a fine battlefield we are leaving here for Rome and Carthage." Have students locate Carthage on the Ancient Italy map on page 12 of *The Story of the Romans*. Explain that in today's reading, they will begin to hear how Pyrrhus' statement was true. Read together *The Story of the Romans*, chapters 42 and 43, "Ancient Ships" and "Regulus and the Snake." Ask for an oral narration.

First Punic War between Rome and Carthage; Rome gains part of Sicily and Corsica (264—241 B.C.)

Grades 7–9: Read together or assign as independent reading *Augustus Caesar's World*, pages 14–21, "Cleopatra and Her Son" and "Caesar's Adopted Son," OR *Beric the Briton*, chapter 3, "A Wolf Hunt," and ask for an oral or written narration.

Grades 10–12: Read together or assign as independent reading *Ben-Hur*, book 5, chapters 7 and 8, "Simonides Renders Account" and "Spiritual or Political?—Simonides Argues."

Lesson 70: Hannibal Crosses the Alps

Materials Needed
- *The Story of the Romans*
- *Mystery of the Roman Ransom* (grades 4–6 or 1–6)
- *Augustus Caesar's World* OR *Beric the Briton* (grades 7–9)
- *Plutarch's Lives* (grades 10–12)

Family: Write "Punic War" on a sheet of paper or small white board for students to see. Ask students what they recall from last time's reading about the First Punic War between Rome and Carthage. Read together *The Story of the Romans*, chapters 44 and 45, "Hannibal Crosses the Alps" and "The Romans Defeated." Ask for an oral narration.

Grades 4–6 or 1–6: Read together or assign as independent reading *Mystery of the Roman Ransom*, chapter 4, "A Surprising Use for Honey."

Grades 7–9: Read together or assign as independent reading *Augustus Caesar's World,* pages 22–28, "Cicero" and "Conspirators Without a Plan," OR *Beric the Briton*, chapter 4, "An Infuriated People," and ask for an oral or written narration.

Grades 10–12: Read together or assign as independent reading about six pages of Plutarch's biography of Antony and ask for an oral or written narration.

Lesson 71: Healing on the Sabbath

Materials Needed
- Bible
- *Foundations in Romans* (grades 7–12)

Family: Ask students what they recall from last time's reading about Jesus' teaching on watchfulness. Explain that His listeners were more focused on the political news, because they wanted someone to save them from Rome. But Jesus continued to focus on heart issues. Read together Luke 13:1–17, John 10:22–42, and Luke 13:31–35 and ask for an oral narration.

Tip: Luke 13:1–5 refers to two historical events: (1) Pilate, the Roman prefect or governor of Judea, killed some Galileans while they were offering sacrifices, and (2) eighteen seemingly innocent bystanders in Siloam were killed when a tower fell on them.

Tip: Herod (Antipas) was the Rome-appointed ruler of the region of Galilee.

Grades 7–12: Begin working on *Foundations in Romans*, lesson 7.

Lesson 72: Jesus at the Pharisee's House; Parables

Materials Needed
- Bible
- *Foundations in Romans* (grades 7–12)

Book of Centuries Timeline

Hannibal crosses the Alps and invades Italy (217 B.C.)

Book of Centuries Timeline

Family: Ask students what they recall from last time's reading about Jesus' teachings and His listeners reactions. Read together Luke 14:1—15:32 and ask for an oral narration.

Grades 7–12: Continue working on *Foundations in Romans*, lesson 7.

Lesson 73: Visit 15 to Europe & Various Readings

Materials Needed
- *Visits to Europe*
- *Mystery of the Roman Ransom* (grades 4–6 or 1–6)
- *The Bronze Bow* (grades 7–9)
- *Ben-Hur* (grades 10–12)

Family: Complete Visit 15 in *Visits to Europe*.

Grades 4–6 or 1–6: Read together or assign as independent reading *Mystery of the Roman Ransom*, chapter 5, "No Respectable Citizen Visits the Cemetery at Night."

Grades 7–9: Read together or assign as independent reading *The Bronze Bow*, chapter 13.

Grades 10–12: Read together or assign as independent reading *Ben-Hur*, book 5, chapters 9 and 10, "Esther and Ben-Hur" and "Posted for the Race."

Lesson 74: The Inventor Archimedes

Materials Needed
- *The Story of the Romans*
- *Augustus Caesar's World* OR *Beric the Briton* (grades 7–9)
- *Ben-Hur* (grades 10–12)

Family: Ask students what they recall from last time's reading about Hannibal, his battles against Rome, and his soldiers' wintering in "the delights of Capua." Read together *The Story of the Romans*, chapter 46, "The Inventor Archimedes." Ask for an oral narration.

Tip: If any of your students read Archimedes and the Door of Science *during the study of Joshua through Malachi & Ancient Greece, ask them to share with the others a bit more about the inventor.*

Carthage makes alliance with Syracuse in Sicily; Rome besieges and takes Syracuse; Archimedes slain (215—211 B.C.)

Grades 7–9: Read together or assign as independent reading *Augustus Caesar's World*, pages 29–34, "Mark Antony," OR *Beric the Briton*, chapter 5, "The Sack of Camalodunum," and ask for an oral or written narration.

Grades 10–12: Read together or assign as independent reading *Ben-Hur*, book 5, chapters 11 and 12, "Making the Wagers" and "The Circus."

Lesson 75: The Roman Conquests

Materials Needed
- *The Story of the Romans*
- *Mystery of the Roman Ransom* (grades 4–6 or 1–6)
- *Augustus Caesar's World* OR *Beric the Briton* (grades 7–9)
- *Plutarch's Lives* (grades 10–12)

Family: Ask students what they recall from last time's reading about Archimedes and Scipio Africanus. Look together at the map on page 14 of *The Story of the Romans* and locate the regions where Rome was waging battles: Spain, Italy, Africa. Locate Macedonia (to the east near Greece) and explain that Roman conquest also began to spread in that direction. Read together *The Story of the Romans*, chapters 47 and 48, "The Roman Conquests" and "Destruction of Carthage." Ask for an oral narration.

Grades 4–6 or 1–6: Read together or assign as independent reading *Mystery of the Roman Ransom*, chapter 6, "A Fateful Letter."

Grades 7–9: Read together or assign as independent reading *Augustus Caesar's World*, pages 35–40, "Why is July?," OR *Beric the Briton*, chapter 6, "First Successes," and ask for an oral or written narration.

Grades 10–12: Read together or assign as independent reading about six pages of Plutarch's biography of Antony and ask for an oral or written narration.

Tip: Make sure older children are up to date with their Discovering Doctrine *notebooks and their Book of Centuries entries.*

Lesson 76: Teachings About This Life and the Next

Materials Needed
- Bible
- *Foundations in Romans* (grades 7–12)

Book of Centuries Timeline

Book of Centuries Timeline

Family: Ask the students what they remember about the parables you read last time. Explain that they will hear more spiritual stories in today's reading. Read together Luke 16:1—17:10 and ask for an oral narration.

Grades 7–12: Continue working on *Foundations in Romans*, lesson 7.

Lesson 77: Jesus Raises Lazarus from the Dead

Materials Needed
- Bible
- *Foundations in Romans* (grades 7–12)

Family: Explain that today's reading is about a deciding moment. When the events read about today occurred, many people made their final decision of what they believed about Jesus. Read together John 11:1–54 and ask for an oral narration.

Grades 7–12: Finish *Foundations in Romans*, lesson 7, this week.

Lesson 78: Visit 16 to Europe & Various Readings

Materials Needed
- *Visits to Europe*
- *Hungry Planet: What the World Eats*
- *Mystery of the Roman Ransom* (grades 4–6 or 1–6)
- *The Bronze Bow* (grades 7–9)
- *Ben-Hur* (grades 10–12)

Family: Complete Visit 16 in *Visits to Europe*.

Grades 4–6 or 1–6: Read together or assign as independent reading *Mystery of the Roman Ransom*, chapter 7, "They All Are in Danger."

Grades 7–9: Read together or assign as independent reading *The Bronze Bow*, chapter 14.

Grades 10–12: Read together or assign as independent reading *Ben-Hur*, book 5, chapters 13 and 14, "The Start" and "The Race."

Lesson 79: Roman Amusements

Materials Needed
- *The Story of the Romans*
- *The Stuff They Left Behind: From the Days of Ancient Rome*
- *Augustus Caesar's World* OR *Beric the Briton* (grades 7–9)
- *Ben-Hur* (grades 10–12)

Family: Display and discuss the picture of the Gladiator Helmet from *The Stuff They Left Behind: From the Days of Ancient Rome*.
   Read together *The Story of the Romans*, chapters 49 and 50, "Roman Amusements" and "The Jewels of Cornelia." Ask for an oral narration.

Grades 7–9: Read together or assign as independent reading *Augustus Caesar's World*, pages 41–45, "Gauls, Geese, and Black Vultures," OR *Beric the Briton*, chapter 7, "Defeat of the Britons," and ask for an oral or written narration.

Grades 10–12: Read together or assign as independent reading *Ben-Hur*, book 5, chapters 15 and 16, "The Invitation of Iras" and "In the Palace of Idernee."

Lesson 80: The Death of Tiberius Gracchus

Materials Needed
- *The Story of the Romans*
- *The Stuff They Left Behind: From the Days of Ancient Rome*
- *Mystery of the Roman Ransom* (grades 4–6 or 1–6)
- *Augustus Caesar's World* OR *Beric the Briton* (grades 7–9)
- *Plutarch's Lives* (grades 10–12)

Family: Display and discuss the picture of the Zilten Mosaic from *The Stuff They Left Behind: From the Days of Ancient Rome*.
   Ask students what they remember from last time's reading about Roman amusements and the jewels of Cornelia. Read together *The Story of the Romans*, chapters 51 and 52, "The Death of Tiberius Gracchus" and "Caius Gracchus." Ask for an oral narration.

Grades 4–6 or 1–6: Read together or assign as independent reading *Mystery of the Roman Ransom*, chapter 8, "He Must Smell of Mimosa."

Grades 7–9: Read together or assign as independent reading *Augustus Caesar's World*, pages 45–49, "Octavian Plays the Game," OR *Beric the Briton*, chapter 8, "The Great Swamps," and ask for an oral or written narration.

Grades 10–12: Read together or assign as independent reading about six pages of Plutarch's biography of Antony and ask for an oral or written narration.

Book of Centuries Timeline

Third Punic War between Rome and Carthage; Carthage defeated (149–146 B.C.)

Rome conquers Corinth and makes Greece a Roman province (146 B.C.)

Spain, previously a colony of Carthage, becomes a Roman province (133 B.C.)

TERM 2

Book of Centuries Timeline

Lesson 81: Ten Lepers Healed; More Parables

Materials Needed
- Bible
- *Foundations in Romans* (grades 7–12)

Family: Ask students what they remember about the deciding event you read about last time. Explain that just as that event changed the lives of Lazarus and his sisters, so the event you will read about today changed the lives of ten men. Read together Luke 17:11—18:14 and ask for an oral narration.

Grades 7–12: Begin working on *Foundations in Romans*, lesson 8.

Lesson 82: The Rich Young Ruler; Blind Bartimaeus

Materials Needed
- Bible
- *Then and Now Bible Maps*
- *Foundations in Romans* (grades 7–12)

Family: Explain that Jesus was on His way to Jerusalem for the Passover Feast and His final week before His crucifixion. Trace his journey on map 12, Holy Land - New Testament, in *Then and Now Bible Maps,* as you read together Mark 10:1–52, then ask for an oral narration.

Tip: These events are also recorded in Matthew 19:1—20:34; Luke 18:15–35. Assign older students to read these parallel passages if desired.

Grades 4–6: Assign your student to read and give a written narration of Mark 10.

Grades 7–12: Continue working on *Foundations in Romans*, lesson 8.

Lesson 83: Visit 17 to Europe & Various Readings

Materials Needed
- *Visits to Europe*
- *Mystery of the Roman Ransom* (grades 4–6 or 1–6)

- *The Bronze Bow* (grades 7–9)
- *Ben-Hur* (grades 10–12)

Family: Complete Visit 17 in *Visits to Europe*.

Grades 4–6 or 1–6: Read together or assign as independent reading *Mystery of the Roman Ransom*, chapter 9, "About Clanging Swords and Grindstones."

Grades 7–9: Read together or assign as independent reading *The Bronze Bow*, chapter 15.

Grades 10–12: Read together or assign as independent reading *Ben-Hur*, book 6, chapters 1 and 2, "The Tower of Antonia—Cell No. VI" and "The Lepers."

Lesson 84: Jugurtha, King of Numidia

Materials Needed
- *The Story of the Romans*
- *The Stuff They Left Behind: From the Days of Ancient Rome*
- *Augustus Caesar's World* OR *Beric the Briton* (grades 7–9)
- *Ben-Hur* (grades 10–12)

Family: Ask students what they recall from last time's reading about Tiberius and Caius Gracchus and their efforts to help the plebeians. Read together *The Story of the Romans*, chapters 53 and 54, "Jugurtha, King of Numidia" and "The Barbarians." Ask for an oral narration.

Display and discuss the picture of the Gundestrup Cauldron from *The Stuff They Left Behind: From the Days of Ancient Rome*.

Grades 7–9: Read together or assign as independent reading *Augustus Caesar's World*, pages 50–55, "Bloody Fingerprints," OR *Beric the Briton*, chapter 9, "The Struggle in the Swamp," and ask for an oral or written narration.

Grades 10–12: Read together or assign as independent reading *Ben-Hur*, book 6, chapters 3 and 4, "Jerusalem Again" and "Ben-Hur at His Father's Gate."

Lesson 85: The Social War

Materials Needed
- *The Story of the Romans*
- *Mystery of the Roman Ransom* (grades 4–6 or 1–6)

Book of Centuries Timeline

Rise of Pharisees and Saducees in Palestine (112 B.C.)

Romans under Marius defeat Jugurtha; Rome expands its provinces in Africa (112–106 B.C.)

Book of Centuries Timeline

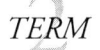

Civil war in the Roman Republic between Marius and Sulla (107–79 B.C.)

- *Augustus Caesar's World* OR *Beric the Briton* (grades 7–9)
- *Plutarch's Lives* (grades 10–12)

Family: Ask students what they recall from last time's reading about the rivalry between Marius, who fought for Rome to the south in Africa, and Sulla, who fought the barbarians in the north. Read together *The Story of the Romans*, chapters 55 and 56, "The Social War" and "The Flight of Marius." Ask for an oral narration.

Grades 4–6 or 1–6: Read together or assign as independent reading *Mystery of the Roman Ransom*, chapter 10, "Hail, Emperor! We, about to Die, Salute You!"

Grades 7–9: Read together or assign as independent reading *Augustus Caesar's World,* pages 56–58, "Candles and Holly Berries," OR *Beric the Briton*, chapter 10, "Betrayed," and ask for an oral or written narration.

Grades 10–12: Read together or assign as independent reading about six pages of Plutarch's biography of Antony and ask for an oral or written narration.

Tip: Make sure older children are up to date with their Discovering Doctrine *notebooks and their Book of Centuries entries.*

Lesson 86: Zacchaeus; Jesus Anointed at Bethany

Materials Needed
- Bible
- *Foundations in Romans* (grades 7–12)

Family: Ask the students what they remember from last time's reading about Jesus' final journey toward Jerusalem. Explain that today's reading will reveal more events that happened along the way. Read together Luke 19:1–27 and John 11:55—12:11 and ask for an oral narration.

Tip: These events are also recorded in Matthew 26:6–13; Mark 14:3–9. Assign older students to read these parallel passages if desired.

Grades 7–12: Continue working on *Foundations in Romans*, lesson 8.

Lesson 87: The Triumphal Entry

Materials Needed
- Bible

- *Foundations in Romans* (grades 7–12)

Family: Ask students what kind of reception they think Jesus might have received in Jerusalem, based on previous readings. Explain that His reception was mixed. Read together Matthew 21:1–46 and ask for an oral narration. Discuss how this Trimphal Entry compares to a Roman Triumph.

Tip: These events are also recorded in Mark 11:1—12:12; Luke 19:29—20:19; John 12:12–19. Assign older students to read these parallel passages if desired.

Grades 4–6: Assign your student to read and give a written narration of Mark 11.

Grades 7–12: Finish *Foundations in Romans*, lesson 8, this week.

Lesson 88: Visit 18 to Europe & Various Readings

Materials Needed
- *Visits to Europe*
- *Mystery of the Roman Ransom* (grades 4–6 or 1–6)
- *The Bronze Bow* (grades 7–9)
- *Ben-Hur* (grades 10–12)

Family: Complete Visit 18 in *Visits to Europe*.

Grades 4–6 or 1–6: Read together or assign as independent reading *Mystery of the Roman Ransom*, chapter 11, "Now We're Back Where We Started."

Grades 7–9: Read together or assign as independent reading *The Bronze Bow*, chapter 16.

Grades 10–12: Read together or assign as independent reading *Ben-Hur*, book 6, chapters 5 and 6, "The Tomb above the King's Garden" and "A Trick of Pilate's—The Combat."

Lesson 89: The Proscription Lists

Materials Needed
- *The Story of the Romans*
- *Augustus Caesar's World* OR *Beric the Briton* (grades 7–9)
- *Ben-Hur* (grades 10–12)

Book of Centuries
Timeline

www.SimplyCharlotteMason.com

TERM 2

Book of Centuries Timeline

Family: Ask students what they recall from last time's reading about the continuing rivalry between Marius and Sulla. Read together *The Story of the Romans*, chapters 57 and 58, "The Proscription Lists" and "Sertorius and His Doe." Ask for an oral narration.

Grades 7–9: Read together or assign as independent reading *Augustus Caesar's World*, pages 59–65, "The Festival of Lights," OR *Beric the Briton*, chapter 11, "A Prisoner," and ask for an oral or written narration.

Grades 10–12: Read together or assign as independent reading *Ben-Hur*, book 7, chapters 1 and 2, "Jerusalem Goes out to a Prophet" and "Nooning by the Pool—Iras."

Lesson 90: The Revolt of the Slaves

Materials Needed
- *The Story of the Romans*
- *Mystery of the Roman Ransom* (grades 4–6 or 1–6)
- *Augustus Caesar's World* OR *Beric the Briton* (grades 7–9)
- *Plutarch's Lives* (grades 10–12)

Family: Ask students what they recall from last time's reading about Sulla's proscription lists in Rome and what became of Marius' friend, Sertorius, in Spain. Read together *The Story of the Romans*, chapters 59 and 60, "The Revolt of the Slaves" and "Pompey's Conquests." Ask for an oral narration.

Revolt of the slaves, led by Spartacus (73—71 B.C.)

Pompey defeats Mithridates and Antiochus of Syria; Syria becomes a Roman province (66—63 B.C.)

Grades 4–6 or 1–6: Read together or assign as independent reading *Mystery of the Roman Ransom*, chapter 12, "Caius Sees the Light."

Grades 7–9: Read together or assign as independent reading *Augustus Caesar's World*, pages 66–70, "Herod, Future King of the Jews," OR *Beric the Briton*, chapter 12, "A School for Gladiators," and ask for an oral or written narration.

Grades 10–12: Read together or assign as independent reading about six pages of Plutarch's biography of Antony and ask for an oral or written narration.

Lesson 91: Parables and Teaching

Materials Needed
- Bible
- *Foundations in Romans* (grades 7–12)

Family: Ask students what they recall about Jesus' mixed reception in Jerusalem during the week before Passover. Explain that in today's reading

64   *www.SimplyCharlotteMason.com*

TERM 2

they will hear four tricky questions: three from the religious rulers who were trying to trick Jesus (verses 15–22, 23–33, and 34–40) and one from Jesus back to the Pharisees (verses 41–46). Read together Matthew 22:1–46. Have students record each of the four questions on a sheet of paper or small white board and narrate the answer that was given.

Tip: These events are also recorded in Mark 12:12–37; Luke 20:20–44. Assign older students to read these parallel passages if desired.

Grades 7–12: Begin working on *Foundations in Romans*, lesson 9.

Lesson 92: Seven Woes; The Widow's Mite

Materials Needed
- Bible
- *Foundations in Romans* (grades 7–12)

Family: Explain that, though Jesus knew the Pharisees were plotting to kill Him, He continued to warn the people about the Pharisees' hypocrisy. Read together Matthew 23:1–39 and Mark 12:41–44 and ask for an oral narration.

Tip: These events are also recorded in Mark 12:38–40; Luke 20:45—21:4. Assign older students to read these parallel passages if desired.

Grades 4–6: Assign your student to read and give a written narration of Mark 12.

Grades 7–12: Continue working on *Foundations in Romans*, lesson 9.

Lesson 93: Visit 19 to Europe & Various Readings

Materials Needed
- *Visits to Europe*
- *Material World*
- *Mystery of the Roman Ransom* (grades 4–6 or 1–6)
- *The Bronze Bow* (grades 7–9)
- *Ben-Hur* (grades 10–12)

Family: Complete Visit 19 in *Visits to Europe*.

Grades 4–6 or 1–6: Read together or assign as independent reading *Mystery of the Roman Ransom*, chapter 13, "Will the City Prefect Call Out His Whole Police Force?"

Book of Centuries Timeline

www.SimplyCharlotteMason.com

Book of Centuries Timeline

Grades 7–9: Read together or assign as independent reading *The Bronze Bow*, chapter 17.

Grades 10–12: Read together or assign as independent reading *Ben-Hur*, book 7, chapters 3 and 4, "The Life of a Soul" and "Ben-Hur Keeps Watch with Iras."

Lesson 94: The Conspiracy of Catiline

Materials Needed
- *The Story of the Romans*
- *Augustus Caesar's World* OR *Beric the Briton* (grades 7–9)
- *Ben-Hur* (grades 10–12)

Family: Ask students what they recall from last time's reading about the revolt of the slaves and Pompey's conquests. Read together *The Story of the Romans*, chapter 61, "The Conspiracy of Catiline." Ask for an oral narration.

Grades 7–9: Read together or assign as independent reading *Augustus Caesar's World*, pages 71–76, "Philippi and the Ghost," OR *Beric the Briton*, chapter 13, "A Christian," and ask for an oral or written narration.

Grades 10–12: Read together or assign as independent reading *Ben-Hur*, book 7, chapter 5, "At Bethabara."

Lesson 95: Caesar's Conquests

Materials Needed
- *The Story of the Romans*
- *The Stuff They Left Behind: From the Days of Ancient Rome*
- *Mystery of the Roman Ransom* (grades 4–6 or 1–6)
- *Augustus Caesar's World* OR *Beric the Briton* (grades 7–9)
- *Plutarch's Lives* (grades 10–12)

Julius Caesar subdues Gaul (France), which becomes a Roman province (58–50 B.C.)

Caesar crosses the Rubicon with an army; civil war between Caesar and Pompey (49 B.C.)

Family: Ask students what they recall from last time's reading about the conspiracy of Catiline and the rise of Julius Caesar in power. Read together *The Story of the Romans*, chapters 62 and 63, "Caesar's Conquests" and "The Crossing of the Rubicon." Ask for an oral narration.

When you read about Crassus' battles with the Parthians, display and discuss the picture of the Parthian Warrior Statue from *The Stuff They Left Behind: From the Days of Ancient Rome*.

Grades 4–6 or 1–6: Read together or assign as independent reading *Mystery of the Roman Ransom*, chapter 14, "The Boys Have No Time to Dive into the Water."

Grades 7–9: Read together or assign as independent reading *Augustus Caesar's World*, pages 77–79, "Antony and Octavian Divide the World," OR *Beric the Briton*, chapter 14, "Rome in Flames," and ask for an oral or written narration.

Grades 10–12: Read together or assign as independent reading about six pages of Plutarch's biography of Antony and ask for an oral or written narration.

Tip: Make sure older children are up to date with their Discovering Doctrine *notebooks and their Book of Centuries entries.*

Lesson 96: Jesus Predicts His Death

Materials Needed
- Bible
- *Foundations in Romans* (grades 7–12)

Family: Ask the students what they recall from previous readings about Jesus' final week in Jerusalem. Explain that it wasn't only the Israelites who knew about Jesus and had to decide whether they believed in Him. Read together John 12:20–38 and ask for an oral narration.

Grades 7–12: Continue working on *Foundations in Romans*, lesson 9.

Lesson 97: Signs of the End of the Age

Materials Needed
- Bible
- *Foundations in Romans* (grades 7–12)

Family: Ask the students what they remember from last time's reading about Jesus' foretelling His death. Explain that in today's reading He foretold what would happen to His disciples. Read together Matthew 24:1–51 and ask for an oral narration.

Tip: These events are also recorded in Mark 13:1–37; Luke 21:5–36. Assign older students to read these parallel passages if desired.

Grades 4–6: Assign your student to read and give a written narration of Mark 13.

Grades 7–12: Finish *Foundations in Romans*, lesson 9, this week.

Book of Centuries Timeline

TERM 2

Book of Centuries Timeline

Lesson 98: Visit 20 to Europe & Various Readings

Materials Needed
- *Visits to Europe*
- *Mystery of the Roman Ransom* (grades 4–6 or 1–6)
- *The Bronze Bow* (grades 7–9)
- *Ben-Hur* (grades 10–12)

Family: Complete Visit 20 in *Visits to Europe*.

Grades 4–6 or 1–6: Read together or assign as independent reading *Mystery of the Roman Ransom*, chapter 15, "The Sieve of the Danaides."

Grades 7–9: Read together or assign as independent reading *The Bronze Bow*, chapter 18.

Grades 10–12: Read together or assign as independent reading *Ben-Hur*, book 8, chapters 1 and 2, "Guests in the House of Hur" and "Ben-Hur Tells of the Nazarene."

Lesson 99: The Battle of Pharsalia

Materials Needed
The Story of the Romans
- *Augustus Caesar's World* OR *Beric the Briton* (grades 7–9)
- *Ben-Hur* (grades 10–12)

Family: Ask students what they recall from last time's reading about Caesar's conquests and the crossing of the Rubicon. Read together *The Story of the Romans*, chapters 64 and 65, "The Battle of Pharsalia" and "The Death of Caesar." Ask for an oral narration.

Grades 7–9: Read together or assign as independent reading *Augustus Caesar's World*, pages 80–84, "Horace and the Country Mouse," OR *Beric the Briton*, chapter 15, "The Christians to the Lions," and ask for an oral or written narration.

Caesar defeats Pompey at Pharsalia and becomes sole dictator (48 B.C.)

Caesar slain on the Ides of March (44 B.C.)

Grades 10–12: Read together or assign as independent reading *Ben-Hur*, book 8, chapters 3 and 4, "The Lepers Leave Their Tomb" and "The Miracle."

Lesson 100: The Second Triumvirate

Materials Needed
- *The Story of the Romans*

- *Mystery of the Roman Ransom* (grades 4–6 or 1–6)
- *Augustus Caesar's World* OR *Beric the Briton* (grades 7–9)
- *Plutarch's Lives* (grades 10–12)

Family: Ask students what they recall from last time's reading about the battle between Pompey and Julius Caesar and their deaths. Read together *The Story of the Romans*, chapters 66 and 67, "The Second Triumvirate" and "The Vision of Brutus." Ask for an oral narration.

Grades 4–6 or 1–6: Read together or assign as independent reading *Mystery of the Roman Ransom*, chapter 16, "Not a Sound Passed Their Lips."

Grades 7–9: Read together or assign as independent reading *Augustus Caesar's World*, pages 84–92, "Antony and Cleopatra" and "Herod, the Fugitive," OR *Beric the Briton*, chapter 16, "In Nero's Palace," and ask for an oral or written narration.

Grades 10–12: Read together or assign as independent reading about six pages of Plutarch's biography of Antony and ask for an oral or written narration.

Lesson 101: Parables of the End of the Age

Materials Needed
- Bible
- *Foundations in Romans* (grades 7–12)

Family: Ask students what they recall from previous readings about Jesus' teachings during this final week. What kinds of things did He talk about and how did He talk about them? Explain that Jesus continued His final teachings by telling more parables in today's reading. Read together Matthew 25:1–46 and ask for an oral narration.

Grades 7–12: Begin working on *Foundations in Romans*, lesson 10.

Lesson 102: The Last Supper

Materials Needed
- Bible
- *Foundations in Romans* (grades 7–12)

Family: Ask students what they recall from last time's reading about Jesus' teachings in parables during His final week. Explain that today's reading marks when Jesus stopped teaching the crowds and focused on His disciples for His remaining hours. Read together Luke 22:1–30 and ask for an oral narration.

Book of Centuries Timeline

TERM 2

Book of Centuries Timeline

Tip: These events are also recorded in Matthew 26:1–20; Mark 14:1–17; John 12:36–50. Assign older students to read these parallel passages if desired.

Grades 7–12: Continue working on *Foundations in Romans*, lesson 10.

Lesson 103: Visit 21 to Europe & Various Readings

Materials Needed
- *Visits to Europe*
- *Mystery of the Roman Ransom* (grades 4–6 or 1–6)
- *The Bronze Bow* (grades 7–9)

Family: Complete Visit 21 in *Visits to Europe*.

Grades 4–6 or 1–6: Read together or assign as independent reading *Mystery of the Roman Ransom*, chapter 17, "Only a Miracle Can Save Caius."

Grades 7–9: Read together or assign as independent reading *The Bronze Bow*, chapter 19.

Lesson 104: Antony and Cleopatra

Materials Needed
- *The Story of the Romans*
- *The Stuff They Left Behind: From the Days of Ancient Rome*
- *Augustus Caesar's World* OR *Beric the Briton* (grades 7–9)
- *Ben-Hur* (grades 10–12)

Family: Ask students what they recall from last time's reading about the events that followed Julius Caesar's death and the Second Triumvirate. Read together *The Story of the Romans*, chapters 68 and 69, "Antony and Cleopatra" and "The Poisonous Snake." Ask for an oral narration.

Display and discuss the Mummy Portrait from Fayum from *The Stuff They Left Behind: From the Days of Ancient Rome*.

Grades 7–9: Read together or assign as independent reading *Augustus Caesar's World*, pages 93–100, "Virgil and Isaiah" and "Octavia Weds Antony," OR *Beric the Briton*, chapter 17, "Betrothal," and ask for an oral or written narration.

Grades 10–12: Read together or assign as independent reading *Ben-Hur*,

Octavius defeats Antony and Cleopatra at Actium; Egypt becomes a Roman province; Octavius assumes title Augustus Caesar, first emperor of Rome (31—30 B.C.)

book 8, chapters 5 and 6, "Pilgrims to the Passover" and "A Serpent of the Nile."

Lesson 105: The Augustan Age

Materials Needed
- *The Story of the Romans*
- *The Stuff They Left Behind: From the Days of Ancient Rome*
- *Mystery of the Roman Ransom* (grades 4–6 or 1–6)
- *Augustus Caesar's World* OR *Beric the Briton* (grades 7–9)
- *Plutarch's Lives* (grades 10–12)

Family: Ask students what they recall from last time's reading about Antony and Cleopatra of Egypt. Display and discuss the picture of the Augustus Statue from *The Stuff They Left Behind: From the Days of Ancient Rome*.
  Read together *The Story of the Romans*, chapters 70 and 71, "The Augustan Age" and "Death of Augustus." Ask for an oral narration.

Grades 4–6 or 1–6: Read together or assign as independent reading *Mystery of the Roman Ransom*, chapter 18, "Memento Mori Is the Password."

Grades 7–9: Read together or assign as independent reading *Augustus Caesar's World*, pages 100–106, "Herod, King of the Jews!" and "To Athens and Return," OR *Beric the Briton*, chapter 18, "The Outbreak," and ask for an oral or written narration.

Grades 10–12: Read together or assign as independent reading about six pages of Plutarch's biography of Antony and ask for an oral or written narration.

Tip: Make sure older children are up to date with their Discovering Doctrine *notebooks and their Book of Centuries entries.*

Lesson 106: Jesus Washes the Disciples' Feet

Materials Needed
- Bible
- *Foundations in Romans* (grades 7–12)

Family: Ask students what they recall from last time's reading about Jesus' final meal with His disciples. Explain that the Apostle John described a part of that final meal that the other Gospel writers did not include. Read together John 13:1–38 and ask for an oral narration.

Book of Centuries Timeline

www.SimplyCharlotteMason.com

TERM 2

Book of Centuries Timeline

Tip: Related events are also recorded in Matthew 26:21–35; Mark 14:18–31; Luke 22:21–38. Assign older students to read these parallel passages if desired.

Grades 4–6: Assign your student to read and give a written narration of Mark 14.

Grades 7–12: Continue working on *Foundations in Romans*, lesson 10.

Lesson 107: Jesus Comforts His Disciples

Materials Needed
- Bible
- *Foundations in Romans* (grades 7–12)

Family: Ask the students what they remember about Jesus' words to the disciples at the Last Supper. Discuss how the disciples might have felt upon hearing those words. Read together John 14:1—15:27 and ask for an oral narration.

Grades 7–12: Finish *Foundations in Romans*, lesson 10, this week.

Lesson 108: Visit 22 to Europe & Various Readings

Materials Needed
- *Visits to Europe*
- *Hungry Planet: What the World Eats*
- *Mystery of the Roman Ransom* (grades 4–6 or 1–6)
- *The Bronze Bow* (grades 7–9)

Family: Complete Visit 22 in *Visits to Europe*.

Grades 4–6 or 1–6: Read together or assign as independent reading *Mystery of the Roman Ransom*, chapter 19, "Everybody Cringes at the Sight of Antonius."

Grades 7–9: Read together or assign as independent reading *The Bronze Bow*, chapter 20.

Lesson 109: Varus Avenged

Materials Needed
- *The Story of the Romans*

- *Augustus Caesar's World* OR *Beric the Briton* (grades 7–9)
- *Ben-Hur* (grades 10–12)

Family: Ask students what they recall from last time's reading about the Age of Augustus. Read together *The Story of the Romans*, chapters 72 and 73, "Varus Avenged" and "Death of Germanicus." Ask for an oral narration.

Grades 7–9: Read together or assign as independent reading *Augustus Caesar's World*, pages 107–111, "The Future Empress" and "The Siege of Jerusalem," OR *Beric the Briton*, chapter 19, "Outlaws," and ask for an oral or written narration.

Grades 10–12: Read together or assign as independent reading *Ben-Hur*, book 8, chapters 7 and 8, "Ben-Hur Returns to Esther" and "Gethsemane—Whom Seek Ye?"

Lesson 110: Tiberius Smothered

Materials Needed
- *The Story of the Romans*
- *The Stuff They Left Behind: From the Days of Ancient Rome*
- *Mystery of the Roman Ransom* (grades 4–6 or 1–6)
- *Augustus Caesar's World* OR *Beric the Briton* (grades 7–9)
- *Plutarch's Lives* (grades 10–12)

Family: Ask students what they recall from last time's reading about Emperor Tiberius and his adopted ward, Germanicus. Read together *The Story of the Romans*, chapter 74, "Tiberius Smothered." Ask for an oral narration.

Display and discuss the picture of the Pantheon from *The Stuff They Left Behind: From the Days of Ancient Rome*.

Grades 4–6 or 1–6: Read together or assign as independent reading *Mystery of the Roman Ransom*, chapter 20, "Riddle upon Riddle."

Grades 7–9: Read together or assign as independent reading *Augustus Caesar's World*, pages 112–116, "A Turning Point," OR *Beric the Briton*, chapter 20, "Mountain Warfare," and ask for an oral or written narration.

Grades 10–12: Read together or assign as independent reading about six pages of Plutarch's biography of Antony and ask for an oral or written narration.

Reminder: If you want to do a hands-on project for lesson 119 or 120, gather any supplies you might need.

Reminder: Start collecting the resources you will need for Term 3. See page 79.

Book of Centuries Timeline

TERM 2

Book of Centuries Timeline

Lesson 111: Jesus Prays for His Disciples

Materials Needed
- Bible
- *Foundations in Romans* (grades 7–12)

Family: Ask the students what they recall from last time's reading about Jesus' final teaching to His disciples. Read together John 16:1—17:26 and ask for an oral narration.

Grades 7–12: Begin working on *Foundations in Romans*, lesson 11.

Lesson 112: Jesus Is Arrested and Tried

Materials Needed
- Bible
- *Foundations in Romans* (grades 7–12)

Family: Ask the students what they remember from last time's reading about Jesus' prayer. Explain that this time of prayer also included Jesus' praying about the crucifixion that He was facing. Read together Luke 22:39–71 and Matthew 27:1–44 and ask for an oral narration.

Tip: These events are also recorded in Matthew 26:36–75; Mark 14:32–72; John 18:1–27; Mark 15:1–32; Luke 23:1–38; John 18:28—19:27. Assign older students to read these parallel passages if desired.

Grades 7–12: Continue working on *Foundations in Romans*, lesson 11.

Lesson 113: Visit 23 to Europe & Various Readings

Materials Needed
- *Visits to Europe*
- *Mystery of the Roman Ransom* (grades 4–6 or 1–6)
- *The Bronze Bow* (grades 7–9)

Family: Complete Visit 23 in *Visits to Europe*.

Grades 4–6 or 1–6: Read together or assign as independent reading *Mystery of the Roman Ransom*, chapter 21, "The Last Straw."

Grades 7–9: Read together or assign as independent reading *The Bronze Bow*, chapter 21.

Tip: Students in grades 7–9 will finish reading The Bronze Bow *next Term.*

Lesson 114: Jesus Is Crucified

Materials Needed
- Bible
- *Augustus Caesar's World* OR *Beric the Briton* (grades 7–9)
- *Ben-Hur* (grades 10–12)

Family: Ask the students what they remember from previous readings about Jesus' trial and crucifixion. Read together Luke 23:39–43, John 19:23–27, and Matthew 27:45–66 and ask for an oral narration.

Tip: These events are also recorded in Mark 15:33–47; Luke 23:44–56; John 19:28–42.

Grades 4–6: Assign your student to read and give a written narration of Mark 15.

Grades 7–9: Read together or assign as independent reading *Augustus Caesar's World*, pages 117–121, "The Love Story Ends," OR *Beric the Briton*, chapter 21, "Old Friends," and ask for an oral or written narration.

Grades 10–12: Read together or assign as independent reading *Ben-Hur*, book 8, chapters 9 and 10, "The Going to Calvary" and "The Crucifixion."

Lesson 115: Jesus' Resurrection

Materials Needed
- Bible
- *Mystery of the Roman Ransom* (grades 4–6 or 1–6)
- *Augustus Caesar's World* OR *Beric the Briton* (grades 7–9)
- *Plutarch's Lives* (grades 10–12)

Family: Ask students what they recall from last time's reading about Jesus' death. Explain that today's reading sets apart Christianity from all other religions. Read together Matthew 28:1–15 and Luke 24:13–49 and ask for an oral narration. Discuss why the Resurrection makes Christianity distinct. (No other religion can claim that its leader is alive today.)

Tip: These events are also recorded in Mark 16:1–14; Luke 24:1–12; John 20:1–23. Assign older students to read these parallel passages if desired.

Grades 4–6 or 1–6: Read together or assign as independent reading *Mystery of the Roman Ransom*, chapter 22, "Thoroughness Sometimes Can Be Pushed Too Far."

Tip: Students in grades 4–6 (or 1–6) will finish Mystery of the Roman Ransom *next Term.*

TERM 2

Book of Centuries Timeline

Jesus Christ crucified (c. 27–33 A.D.)

Book of Centuries Timeline

Grades 7–9: Read together or assign as independent reading *Augustus Caesar's World*, pages 122–128, "Herod and Mariamne" and "Triumph and Peace," if reading this book, and ask for an oral or written narration. Or use today to catch up on any assigned reading from *Beric the Briton* as needed.

Grades 10–12: Read together or assign as independent reading the rest of Plutarch's biography of Antony and ask for an oral or written narration.

Tip: Make sure older children are up to date with their Discovering Doctrine *notebooks and their Book of Centuries entries.*

Lesson 116: Bible Exam or Catch Up

Materials Needed
- Bible (if doing catch-up reading)
- *Foundations in Romans* (grades 7–12)

Family: Use this day to catch up on any Bible reading you need to finish, or use the questions below for the students' exam on the Life of Christ studied so far.
Grades 1–3: Tell the story of the Good Samaritan.
Grades 4–6: Tell a parable about the kingdom of heaven.
Grades 7–9: "I am the resurrection and the life." Tell all you can remember about Who said this to whom and the circumstances surrounding it.
Grades 10–12: What did Jesus say is the greatest and the second commandment and why? Explain how that statement is true and contrast it to the Pharisees' view of the commandments.

Grades 7–12: Continue working on *Foundations in Romans*, lesson 11.

Lesson 117: Bible Exam or Catch Up

Materials Needed
- Bible (if doing catch-up reading)
- *Foundations in Romans* (grades 7–12)

Family: Use this day to catch up on any Bible reading you need to finish, or use the questions below for the students' exam on the Life of Christ studied so far.
Grades 1–3: Tell the story of Zacchaeus the tax collector.
Grades 4–6: Tell how Jesus was received when He entered Jerusalem for the final time.
Grades 7–9: Describe Peter, Jesus' disciple, in full, citing accounts and what you can learn about him from those events.

Grades 10–12: Explain in full Pilate's role in Jesus' death.

Grades 7–12: Finish *Foundations in Romans*, lesson 11, this week.
   Select a chapter from Romans 6–11 and ask for a narration. Allow the student to look at the chapter outline in *Foundations in Romans* if necessary.

Lesson 118: Visit 24 to Europe

Materials Needed
- *Visits to Europe*

Family: Complete Visit 24 in *Visits to Europe*.

Lesson 119: Ancient Rome Catch Up, Project, or Exam

Materials Needed
- *The Story of the Romans,* if needed
- (optional) Materials for hands-on project

Family: Use this day to catch up on any history reading you need to finish, or use the questions below for the students' exam on their Ancient Rome readings. You may also use this lesson and the next to do an optional hands-on project if you would prefer.
Grades 1–3: Tell the story of Julius Caesar.
Grades 4–6: Tell the story of Scipio Africanus and Hannibal, including Hannibal's reply to the question, "Who do you think is the greatest general that ever lived."
Grades 7–9: Tell all you know about Cornelia and her two "jewels."
Grades 10–12: Tell in full about the Punic Wars.

Optional Hands-On Project: Select a hands-on project from the Links and Tips page at http://simplycm.com/matthew-links.

Lesson 120: Ancient Rome Catch Up, Project, or Exam

Materials Needed
- *The Story of the Romans,* if needed
- (optional) Materials for hands-on project

Family: Use this day to catch up on any history reading you need to finish,

Book of Centuries Timeline

Book of Centuries Timeline

or use the questions below for the students' exam on their Ancient Rome readings. You may also do an optional hands-on project.

Grades 1–3: Tell the story of another Roman emperor of whom you read this term.

Grades 4–6: Tell all you can remember about Antony, Cleopatra, and Octavius.

Grades 7–9: Describe three other events that were happening in the world during the life of Caesar Augustus.

Grades 10–12: Describe the character of Antony, citing examples from his life story.

Optional Hands-On Project: Continue your selected hands-on project or start a new one if desired.

Term 3
(12 weeks; 5 lessons/week)

Term 3 Book List
Family
- Bible
- *City* by David Macaulay
- *Material World* **and** *Hungry Planet: What the World Eats* by Peter Menzel
- *Peril and Peace* by Mindy and Brandon Withrow
- *The Roman Colosseum* by Elizabeth Mann
- *The Story of the Romans* by H. A. Guerber, edited by Christine Miller (Nothing New Press edition)
- *The Stuff They Left Behind: From the Days of Ancient Rome* portfolio
- *Then and Now Bible Maps* from Rose Publishing
- *Visits to Europe* notebook (one for each student)

Plus . . .
Grades 1–3
- *Mystery of the Roman Ransom* by Henry Winterfeld (if desired)

Grades 4–6
- *Galen and the Gateway to Medicine* by Jeanne Bendick
- *Mystery of the Roman Ransom* by Henry Winterfeld

Grades 7–9
- *Augustus Caesar's World* by Genevieve Foster
  OR *For the Temple* by G. A. Henty
- Book of Centuries (one for each student)
- *The Bronze Bow* by Elizabeth George Speare
- *Discovering Doctrine* by Sonya Shafer (one for each student)
- *Foundations in Romans: A Romans Bible Study* by Sonya Shafer (one for each student)

Grades 10–12
- *The Apostle: A Life of Paul* by John Pollock
- *Augustus Caesar's World* by Genevieve Foster
- Book of Centuries (one for each student)
- *Discovering Doctrine* by Sonya Shafer (one for each student)
- *Foundations in Romans: A Romans Bible Study* by Sonya Shafer (one for each student)
- *Peril and Peace* by Mindy and Brandon Withrow

Optional
- Various resources for hands-on projects

What You Will Cover As a Family

Bible: The book of Acts

Geography: Europe, with special emphasis on Germany and Poland

History: Ancient Rome, from Emperor Caligula to the fall of the Roman Empire

Term 3 At a Glance

	Family	Grades 1–3	Grades 4–6	Grades 7–9	Grades 10–12
\multicolumn{6}{c}{**Week 1, Lessons 121–125**}
Bible	Life of Christ		Mark Study	Romans Study, lesson 12	Romans Study lesson 12; The Apostle, ch. 1, 2
Geography	Visits to Europe, Visit 25				
History	The Story of the Romans, ch. 75–77		Mystery of the Roman Ransom, ch. 23, 24	Bronze Bow, ch. 22; Augustus Caesar's World OR For the Temple, ch. 1, 2	Augustus Caesar's World
\multicolumn{6}{c}{**Week 2, Lessons 126–130**}
Bible	Acts			Romans Study, lesson 12	Romans Study, lesson 12; The Apostle, ch. 3–8
Geography	Visits to Europe, Visit 26				
History			Mystery of the Roman Ransom, ch. 25	Bronze Bow, ch. 23; Augustus Caesar's World OR For the Temple, ch. 3, 4	Augustus Caesar's World
\multicolumn{6}{c}{**Week 3, Lessons 131–135**}
Bible	Acts			Romans Study, lesson 13	Romans Study, lesson 13; The Apostle, ch. 9–14
Geography	Visits to Europe, Visit 27				
History			Mystery of the Roman Ransom, Catch Up	Bronze Bow, ch. 24; Augustus Caesar's World OR For the Temple, ch. 5, 6	Augustus Caesar's World
\multicolumn{6}{c}{**Week 4, Lessons 136–140**}
Bible	Acts			Romans Study, lesson 13	Romans Study, lesson 13; The Apostle, ch. 15–20
Geography	Visits to Europe, Visit 28				
History	City		Galen and the Gateway to Medicine, ch. 1, 2	Augustus Caesar's World OR For the Temple, ch. 7, 8	Augustus Caesar's World
\multicolumn{6}{c}{**Week 5, Lessons 141–145**}
Bible	Acts			Romans Study, lesson 14	Romans Study, lesson 14; The Apostle, ch. 21–26
Geography	Visits to Europe, Visit 29				
History			Galen and the Gateway to Medicine, ch. 3, 4A	Augustus Caesar's World OR For the Temple, ch. 9, 10	Augustus Caesar's World
\multicolumn{6}{c}{**Week 6, Lessons 146–150**}
Bible	Acts			Romans Study, lesson 14	Romans Study, lesson 14; The Apostle, ch. 27–32
Geography	Visits to Europe, Visit 30				
History			Galen and the Gateway to Medicine, ch. 4B, 5	Augustus Caesar's World OR For the Temple, ch. 11, 12	Augustus Caesar's World

Use this chart to see what your family and each of your students will be studying week by week during this term. You will also be able to see when each book is scheduled to be used.

TERM 3

	Family	Grades 1–3	Grades 4–6	Grades 7–9	Grades 10–12
Week 7, Lessons 151–155					
Bible	Acts			Romans Study, lesson 15	Romans Study, lesson 15 ; The Apostle, ch. 33–36
Geography	Visits to Europe, Visit 31				
History	Story of the Romans, ch. 78–81; The Roman Colosseum		Galen and the Gateway to Medicine, ch. 6, 7	Augustus Caesar's World OR For the Temple, ch. 13, 14	Augustus Caesar's World
Week 8, Lessons 156–160					
Bible				Romans Study, lesson 15	Romans Study, lesson 15
Geography	Visits to Europe, Visit 32				
History	The Roman Colosseum; Story of the Romans, ch. 82–86; Peril and Peace, Polycarp		Galen and the Gateway to Medicine, ch. 8, 9	Augustus Caesar's World OR For the Temple, ch. 15, 16	Augustus Caesar's World; Peril and Peace
Week 9, Lessons 161–165					
Bible				Romans Study, lesson 16	Romans Study, lesson 16
Geography	Visits to Europe, Visit 33				
History	Story of the Romans, ch. 87–94; Peril and Peace, Origen		Galen and the Gateway to Medicine, ch. 10	Augustus Caesar's World OR For the Temple, ch. 17, 18	Augustus Caesar's World; Peril and Peace
Week 10, Lessons 166–170					
Bible				Romans Study, lesson 16	Romans Study, lesson 16
Geography	Visits to Europe, Visit 34				
History	Story of the Romans, ch. 95–100; Peril and Peace, Athanasius		Galen and the Gateway to Medicine, ch. 11, 12	Augustus Caesar's World OR For the Temple, ch. 19	Augustus Caesar's World; Peril and Peace
Week 11, Lessons 171–175					
Bible				Romans Study, lesson 17	Romans Study, lesson 17
Geography	Visits to Europe, Visit 35				
History	Peril and Peace, Ambrose, Augustine, Jerome; Story of the Romans, ch. 101, 102		Galen and the Gateway to Medicine, ch. 13	Augustus Caesar's World	Augustus Caesar's World; Peril and Peace
Week 12, Lessons 176–180					
Bible	Exam or Catch Up			Romans Study, lesson 17	Romans Study, lesson 17
Geography	Visits to Europe, Visit 36				
History	Catch Up or Project or Exam				(opt.) Peril and Peace

Lesson 121: Jesus Appears to His Disciples

Materials Needed
- Bible
- *Foundations in Romans* (grades 7–12)

Family: Ask the students what they recall from last time's reading about Jesus' resurrection and appearance to His disciples. Read together John 20:24–29 and John 21:1–24 and ask for an oral narration.

Tip: These events are also recorded in Mark 16:12–18. Assign older students to read this parallel passage if desired.

Grades 7–12: Begin working on *Foundations in Romans*, lesson 12.

Lesson 122: Jesus Ascends to Heaven

Materials Needed
- Bible
- *Then and Now Bible Maps*
- *Foundations in Romans* (grades 7–12)

Family: Ask the students what they remember about Jesus' appearances after His resurrection. Explain that today's reading will contain His final words to His disciples here on earth. Read together Matthew 28:16–20 and Acts 1:1–11. Together locate on map 12, Holy Land - New Testament, in *Then and Now Bible Maps* the regions Jesus mentioned in His command. (Jerusalem, Judea, Samaria, ends of the earth.)

Read John 20:30 and 31 and John 21:25 and ask for an oral narration on Jesus' last instructions. Then read Acts 1:12–26 and ask for an oral narration on the disciples' actions.

Tip: These events are also recorded in Mark 16:19, 20; Luke 24:50–53. Assign older students to read these parallel passages if desired.

Grades 4–6: Assign your student to read and give a written narration of Mark 16.

Grades 7–12: Continue working on *Foundations in Romans*, lesson 12.

Lesson 123: Visit 25 to Europe & Various Readings

Materials Needed
- *Visits to Europe*

Book of Centuries Timeline

TERM 3

www.SimplyCharlotteMason.com

83

Book of Centuries Timeline

- *Mystery of the Roman Ransom* (grades 4–6 or 1–6)
- *The Bronze Bow* (grades 7–9)
- *The Apostle: A Life of Paul* (grades 10–12)

Family: Complete Visit 25 in *Visits to Europe*.

Grades 4–6 or 1–6: Read together or assign as independent reading *Mystery of the Roman Ransom*, chapter 23, "A Distressing Turn of Events."

Grades 7–9: Read together or assign as independent reading *The Bronze Bow*, chapter 22.

Grades 10–12: Read together or assign as independent reading *The Apostle: A Life of Paul*, chapters 1 and 2, "From the Land of Black Tents" and "Stephen."

Lesson 124: The Wild Caligula

Materials Needed
- *The Story of the Romans*
- *The Stuff They Left Behind: From the Days of Ancient Rome*
- *Augustus Caesar's World* OR *For the Temple* (grades 7–9)
- *Augustus Caesar's World* (grades 10–12)

Family: Display and discuss the picture of the Aqua Claudia Aqueduct from *The Stuff They Left Behind: From the Days of Ancient Rome*. Explain that this aqueduct was begun by Caligula and finished by Claudius, both of whom you will read about today.
Read together *The Story of the Romans*, chapters 75 and 76, "The Wild Caligula" and "The Wicked Wives of Claudius." Ask for an oral narration.

Rome defeats Caractacus in Britain; Britain becomes a Roman province (A.D. 43)

Grades 7–9: Read together or assign as independent reading *Augustus Caesar's World*, pages 129–140, "Augustus Caesar!" and "The Druids," OR *For the Temple*, chapter 1, "The Lake of Tiberias," and ask for an oral or written narration.

Grades 10–12: Read together or assign as independent reading *Augustus Caesar's World*, pages xi–13, "Introduction" through "The Ides of March," and ask for an oral or written narration.

Lesson 125: Nero's First Crimes

Materials Needed
- *The Story of the Romans*
- *The Stuff They Left Behind: From the Days of Ancient Rome*
- *Mystery of the Roman Ransom* (grades 4–6 or 1–6)
- *Augustus Caesar's World* OR *For the Temple* (grades 7–9)
- *Augustus Caesar's World* (grades 10–12)

Family: Ask students what they recall from last time's reading about the cruel Caligula and his successor, Claudius. Read together *The Story of the Romans*, chapter 77, "Nero's First Crimes." Ask for an oral narration.

Display and discuss the picture of Roman Coins from *The Stuff They Left Behind: From the Days of Ancient Rome*.

Grades 4–6 or 1–6: Read together or assign as independent reading *Mystery of the Roman Ransom*, chapter 24, "How Much Does a Bear Weigh?"

Grades 7–9: Read together or assign as independent reading *Augustus Caesar's World*, pages 141–146, "Tales of the Wild Northwest" and "A Wedding," OR *For the Temple*, chapter 2, "A Storm on Galilee," and ask for an oral or written narration.

Grades 10–12: Read together or assign as independent reading *Augustus Caesar's World*, pages 14–28, "Cleopatra and Her Son" through "Conspirators Without a Plan," and ask for an oral or written narration.

Tip: Make sure older children are up to date with their Discovering Doctrine *notebooks and their Book of Centuries entries.*

Book of Centuries Timeline

Lesson 126: Many Believe at Pentecost

Materials Needed
- Bible
- *Foundations in Romans* (grades 7–12)
- *The Apostle: A Life of Paul* (grades 10–12)

Family: Ask the students what they recall about what the disciples did after Jesus ascended into Heaven. Explain that another annual feast arrived soon, Pentecost, and people from all over Judea (and the world) came to Jerusalem again. This gathering set the stage for the next step of God's plan for His church. Read together Acts 2:1–47 and ask for an oral narration.

Grades 7–12: Continue working on *Foundations in Romans*, lesson 12.

Grades 10–12: Read together or assign as independent reading *The Apostle: A Life of Paul*, chapters 3 and 4, "Damascus Road" and "A Man Surprised."

Lesson 127: Peter and John Preach

Materials Needed
- Bible
- *Foundations in Romans* (grades 7–12)
- *The Apostle: A Life of Paul* (grades 10–12)

Book of Centuries Timeline

Family: Ask the students what they remember from last time's reading about old and new disciples/believers. Explain that in today's reading they will see how Peter had changed since the Resurrection and the coming of the Holy Spirit. Read together Acts 3:1—4:31 and ask for an oral narration. Discuss how Peter no longer hid his faith in Jesus, but showed boldness.

Grades 7–12: Finish working on *Foundations in Romans*, lesson 12, this week.

Grades 10–12: Read together or assign as independent reading *The Apostle: A Life of Paul*, chapters 5 and 6, "Arabia and After" and "Hidden Years."

Reminder: Get *Galen and the Gateway to Medicine* for grades 4–6 and *City* for Family for lessons 137 and 138.

Lesson 128: Visit 26 to Europe & Various Readings

Materials Needed
- *Visits to Europe*
- *Mystery of the Roman Ransom* (grades 4–6 or 1–6)
- *The Bronze Bow* (grades 7–9)
- *The Apostle: A Life of Paul* (grades 10–12)

Family: Complete Visit 26 in *Visits to Europe*.

Grades 4–6 or 1–6: Read together or assign as independent reading *Mystery of the Roman Ransom*, chapter 25, "Caius Sees Another Light."

Grades 7–9: Read together or assign as independent reading *The Bronze Bow*, chapter 23.

Grades 10–12: Read together or assign as independent reading *The Apostle: A Life of Paul*, chapters 7 and 8, "The New Era" and "Aphrodite's Island."

Lesson 129: Ananias and Sapphira

Materials Needed
- Bible
- *Augustus Caesar's World* OR *For the Temple* (grades 7–9)
- *Augustus Caesar's World* (grades 10–12)

Family: Ask the students what they recall from last time's reading about Peter and John and their run-in with the council of religious leaders. Explain that God was taking care of this early church, protecting it from outside and inside. Read together Acts 4:32—5:42 and ask for an oral narration.

Tip: The Roman Empire was in charge of Israel at this point in history. They had authority over civil disputes, but the Jewish religious leaders still had authority over matters that pertained to their religious law. The Sanhedrin was a group of Pharisees and Saducees that decided such religious matters.

Grades 7–9: Read together or assign as independent reading *Augustus Caesar's World*, pages 147–154, "The Pantheon" and "A Bible for the Romans," OR *For the Temple*, chapter 3, "The Revolt Against Rome," and ask for an oral or written narration.

Grades 10–12: Read together or assign as independent reading *Augustus Caesar's World*, pages 29–45, "Mark Antony" through "Gauls, Geese, and Black Vultures," and ask for an oral or written narration.

Lesson 130: Stephen Is Stoned

Materials Needed
- Bible
- *Then and Now Bible Maps*
- *Augustus Caesar's World* OR *For the Temple* (grades 7–9)
- *Augustus Caesar's World* (grades 10–12)

Family: Ask the students what they remember from last time's reading about the believers and how they related to each other. Explain that different challenges faced those believers as their numbers grew. Read together Acts 6:1—8:4 and ask for an oral narration.

Have the students locate on map 12, Holy Land - New Testament, in *Then and Now Bible Maps* the regions where the disciples were scattered.

Grades 7–9: Read together or assign as independent reading *Augustus Caesar's World*, pages 155–165, "The Story of Aeneas" and "Who Were the Roman Gods?," OR *For the Temple*, chapter 4, "The Lull Before the Storm," and ask for an oral or written narration.

Grades 10–12: Read together or assign as independent reading *Augustus Caesar's World*, pages 45–58, "Octavian Plays the Game" through "Candles and Holly Berries," and ask for an oral or written narration.

Lesson 131: Philip and the Ethiopian

Materials Needed
- Bible

Book of Centuries Timeline

- *Foundations in Romans* (grades 7–12)
- *The Apostle: A Life of Paul* (grades 10–12)

Family: Ask the students what they remember from last time's reading about the believers' being scattered. Explain that their scattering was not a mistake, but part of God's plan to continue to spread the gospel of Jesus Christ. Read together Acts 8:5–40 and ask for an oral narration.

Grades 7–12: Begin working on *Foundations in Romans*, lesson 13.

Grades 10–12: Read together or assign as independent reading *The Apostle: A Life of Paul*, chapters 9 and 10, "Into Galatia" and "Progress and Persecution."

Lesson 132: Saul Becomes a Believer

Materials Needed
- Bible
- *Then and Now Bible Maps*
- *Foundations in Romans* (grades 7–12)
- *The Apostle: A Life of Paul* (grades 10–12)

Family: Briefly remind the students how the gospel was starting to spread because of the disciples' being scattered and because of Philip's traveling and preaching. Explain that today's account will show how the gospel had spread even farther. Read together Acts 9:1–31 and ask for an oral narration.
  Have students locate Damascus on map 12, Holy Land - New Testament, in *Then and Now Bible Maps* and estimate how many miles the gospel had been spread at this time. (Use the mile key at the bottom of the map to help with the estimate.)

Grades 7–12: Continue working on *Foundations in Romans*, lesson 13.

Grades 10–12: Read together or assign as independent reading *The Apostle: A Life of Paul*, chapters 11 and 12, "Stoned" and "I Opposed Him to His Face."

Lesson 133: Visit 27 to Europe & Various Readings

Materials Needed
- *Visits to Europe*
- *Material World*
- *Mystery of the Roman Ransom,* if needed (grades 4–6 or 1–6)
- *The Bronze Bow* (grades 7–9)
- *The Apostle: A Life of Paul* (grades 10–12)

Family: Complete Visit 27 in *Visits to Europe*.

Grades 4–6 or 1–6: Use today to finish any assigned reading in *Mystery of the Roman Ransom*.

Grades 7–9: Read together or assign as independent reading *The Bronze Bow*, chapter 24.

Grades 10–12: Read together or assign as independent reading *The Apostle: A Life of Paul*, chapters 13 and 14, "Dear Idiots of Galatia" and "A Fresh Start."

Lesson 134: The Gospel Goes to the Gentiles

Materials Needed
- Bible
- *Then and Now Bible Maps*
- *Augustus Caesar's World* OR *For the Temple* (grades 7–9)
- *Augustus Caesar's World* (grades 10–12)

Family: Ask the students what they recall from last time's reading about Saul and what happened to him on his trip to Damascus. Explain that while Saul was preaching in Jerusalem and Tarsus, Peter was spreading the gospel elsewhere. Read together Acts 9:32—10:48 and ask for an oral narration.
   Together locate Joppa and Caesarea on map 12, Holy Land - New Testament, in *Then and Now Bible Maps*.

Grades 7–9: Read together or assign as independent reading *Augustus Caesar's World*, pages 166–176, "Golden Eagles Come Home," "Out of Persia," and "We Still Call It Sunday," OR *For the Temple*, chapter 5, "The Siege of Jotapata," and ask for an oral or written narration.

Grades 10–12: Read together or assign as independent reading *Augustus Caesar's World*, pages 59–76, "The Festival of Lights" through "Philippi and the Ghost," and ask for an oral or written narration.

Lesson 135: Peter's Explanation and Escape

Materials Needed
- Bible
- *Then and Now Bible Maps*
- *Augustus Caesar's World* OR *For the Temple* (grades 7–9)
- *Augustus Caesar's World* (grades 10–12)

*Book of Centuries
Timeline*

TERM 3

Book of Centuries Timeline

Family: Ask the students what they remember from last time's reading about Peter and Cornelius. Read together Acts 11:1–30 and ask for an oral narration.

Show map 12, Holy Land - New Testament, in *Then and Now Bible Maps* and explain that by this time the disciples had scattered and taken the gospel farther than this map shows. Turn to map 15, Paul's Journeys, and have students locate Jerusalem first, where it all started, then the regions (in pink) mentioned in verse 19.

Read together Acts 12:1–25 and ask for an oral narration.

Grades 7–9: Read together or assign as independent reading *Augustus Caesar's World*, pages 177–185, "Herod and the Temple" and "Hillel, the Great Pharisee," OR *For the Temple*, chapter 6, "The Fall of the City," and ask for an oral or written narration.

Grades 10–12: Read together or assign as independent reading *Augustus Caesar's World*, pages 77–90, "Antony and Octavian Divide the World" through "Antony and Cleopatra," and ask for an oral or written narration.

Tip: Make sure older children are up to date with their *Discovering Doctrine* notebooks and their Book of Centuries entries.

Lesson 136: Barnabas and Paul Start Off

Materials Needed
- Bible
- *Then and Now Bible Maps,* dry erase marker
- *Foundations in Romans* (grades 7–12)
- *The Apostle: A Life of Paul* (grades 10–12)

Family: Ask the students what they remember from last time's reading about James' death and Peter's imprisonment. Also review what Barnabas and Saul had been doing (11:19–30). Explain that today's reading will pick up the narrative of Barnabas and Saul again. Read together Acts 13:1–12 and ask for an oral narration.

In *Then and Now Bible Maps*, flip the plastic "Now" map (14) over to cover the Paul's Journeys map (15) and have the students use a dry erase marker to trace where Paul and Barnabas went to share the gospel message. Read together Acts 13:13–52 and trace those locations also.

Grades 7–12: Continue working on *Foundations in Romans*, lesson 13.

Grades 10–12: Read together or assign as independent reading *The Apostle: A Life of Paul*, chapters 15 and 16, "Across to Europe" and "Flogged in Philippi."

Lesson 137: City

Materials Needed
- City
- *Foundations in Romans* (grades 7–12)
- *The Apostle: A Life of Paul* (grades 10–12)

Family: Ask students what they recall about Paul and Barnabas' travels so far. Remind students that those men were traveling to various cities in the Roman Empire. Read together *City*, pages 7–43.

Grades 7–12: Finish working on *Foundations in Romans*, lesson 13, this week.

Grades 10–12: Read together or assign as independent reading *The Apostle: A Life of Paul*, chapters 17 and 18, "Thrown Out of Thessalonica" and "The Fugitive."

Lesson 138: Visit 28 to Europe & Various Readings

Materials Needed
- *Visits to Europe*
- *Galen and the Gateway to Medicine* (grades 4–6)
- *The Apostle: A Life of Paul* (grades 10–12)

Family: Complete Visit 28 in *Visits to Europe*.

Grades 4–6: Read together or assign as independent reading *Galen and the Gateway to Medicine*, chapter 1, "Who Was Galen?," and ask for an oral or written narration.

Grades 10–12: Read together or assign as independent reading *The Apostle: A Life of Paul*, chapters 19 and 20, "Laughter in Athens" and "City of Unbridled Love."

Lesson 139: City (continued)

Materials Needed
- City
- *Augustus Caesar's World* OR *For the Temple* (grades 7–9)
- *Augustus Caesar's World* (grades 10–12)

Family: Read together *City*, pages 44–81.

Grades 7–9: Read together or assign as independent reading *Augustus*

Book of Centuries Timeline

TERM 3

Book of Centuries Timeline

Caesar's World, pages 186–194, "The Law of Moses" and "Augustus, the God," OR *For the Temple*, chapter 7, "The Massacre on the Lake," and ask for an oral or written narration.

Grades 10–12: Read together or assign as independent reading *Augustus Caesar's World*, pages 91–106, "Herod, the Fugitive" through "To Athens and Return," and ask for an oral or written narration.

Lesson 140: City (concluded)

Materials Needed
- *City*
- *Galen and the Gateway to Medicine* (grades 4–6)
- *Augustus Caesar's World* OR *For the Temple* (grades 7–9)
- *Augustus Caesar's World* (grades 10–12)

Family: Read together *City*, pages 82–111.

Grades 4–6: Read together or assign as independent reading *Galen and the Gateway to Medicine*, chapter 2, "Galen's World," and ask for an oral or written narration.

Grades 7–9: Read together or assign as independent reading *Augustus Caesar's World*, pages 195–204, "A Roman Pharaoh," OR *For the Temple*, chapter 8, "Among the Mountains," and ask for an oral or written narration.

Grades 10–12: Read together or assign as independent reading *Augustus Caesar's World*, pages 107–121, "The Future Empress" through "The Love Story Ends," and ask for an oral or written narration.

Lesson 141: Reporting on God's Work

Materials Needed
- Bible
- *Then and Now Bible Maps,* dry erase marker
- *Foundations in Romans* (grades 7–12)
- *The Apostle: A Life of Paul* (grades 10–12)

First council of apostles at Jerusalem (50)

Family: Ask the students what they recall about Paul and Barnabas' travels and the receptions they were experiencing in the various cities. Read together Acts 14:1–28 and have the students add those locations to the Paul's Journeys map overlay (14) in *Then and Now Bible Maps*, using a dry erase marker. Ask them to estimate how many miles the gospel had spread at this point.

Book of Centuries Timeline

Read together Acts 15:1–35 and ask for an oral narration.

Grades 7–12: Begin working on *Foundations in Romans*, lesson 14.

Grades 10–12: Read together or assign as independent reading *The Apostle: A Life of Paul*, chapters 21 and 22, "The House of Gaius" and "Gallio's Decision."

Lesson 142: Paul and Silas Travel

Materials Needed
- Bible
- *Then and Now Bible Maps,* dry erase marker
- *Foundations in Romans* (grades 7–12)
- *The Apostle: A Life of Paul* (grades 10–12)

Family: Ask the students what they remember from last time's reading about Paul's first missionary journey. Read together Acts 15:36—16:40 and ask for an oral narration. Have the students trace the locations of Paul's second missionary journey on the map 14 overlay in *Then and Now Bible Maps* as you read about them. You may want to erase the marks from the first journey or use a different color to trace this second journey.

Grades 7–12: Continue working on *Foundations in Romans*, lesson 14.

Grades 10–12: Read together or assign as independent reading *The Apostle: A Life of Paul*, chapters 23 and 24, "A School at Ephesus" and "The Name."

Tip: The chapters read today in The Apostle *describe the image of Diana of the Ephesians, a picture of which is included in* The Stuff They Left Behind: From the Days of Ancient Rome. *You will have the option to display and discuss that picture with the whole family in lesson 146 if you think it would be suitable for all your children to see. Alternately, you could allow your grades 10–12 students to look at it as they read the description in Pollock's book.*

Lesson 143: Visit 29 to Europe & Various Readings

Materials Needed
- *Visits to Europe*
- *Hungry Planet: What the World Eats*
- *Galen and the Gateway to Medicine* (grades 4–6)
- *The Apostle: A Life of Paul* (grades 10–12)

Book of Centuries Timeline

Family: Complete Visit 29 in *Visits to Europe*.

Grades 4–6: Read together or assign as independent reading *Galen and the Gateway to Medicine*, chapter 3, "Galen Goes to School," and ask for an oral or written narration.

Grades 10–12: Read together or assign as independent reading *The Apostle: A Life of Paul*, chapters 25 and 26, "The Happiest Letter" and "The Greatest of These."

Lesson 144: The Gospel in Greece

Materials Needed
- Bible
- *Then and Now Bible Maps,* dry erase marker
- *Augustus Caesar's World* OR *For the Temple* (grades 7–9)
- *Augustus Caesar's World* (grades 10–12)

Family: Ask the students to recall from last time's reading events of Paul's second missionary journey so far. Read together Acts 17:1—18:22 and ask for an oral narration. Have the students trace the final stops on Paul's second missionary journey onto the map 14 overlay in *Then and Now Bible Maps* as you read about them.

Grades 7–9: Read together or assign as independent reading *Augustus Caesar's World*, pages 205–214, "Remember Akhenaton" and "Philo and the Lighthouse," OR *For the Temple*, chapter 9, "The Storming of Gamala," and ask for an oral or written narration.

Grades 10–12: Read together or assign as independent reading *Augustus Caesar's World*, pages 122–136, "Herod and Mariamne" through "Augustus Caesar!," and ask for an oral or written narration.

Lesson 145: A Riot in Ephesus

Materials Needed
- Bible
- *The Stuff They Left Behind: From the Days of Ancient Rome*
- *Then and Now Bible Maps*, dry erase marker
- *Galen and the Gateway to Medicine* (grades 4–6)
- *Augustus Caesar's World* OR *For the Temple* (grades 7–9)
- *Augustus Caesar's World* (grades 10–12)

Family: Display and discuss the picture of the Athens Agora Idols from *The Stuff They Left Behind: From the Days of Ancient Rome*.

Book of Centuries Timeline

Ask the students what they remember about Paul's second missionary journey and his stop in Athens. Read together Acts 18:23—20:1 and ask for an oral narration.

Have the students trace the stops on Paul's third missionary journey onto the map 14 overlay in *Then and Now Bible Maps* as you read about them. You may want to erase the marks from the other journeys or use a different color to specify this journey on the map.

Grades 4–6: Read together or assign as independent reading *Galen and the Gateway to Medicine*, the first half of chapter 4, "Galen Begins to Study Medicine," pages 25–31, and ask for an oral or written narration.

Grades 7–9: Read together or assign as independent reading *Augustus Caesar's World*, pages 215–223, "Questions and Answers," OR *For the Temple*, chapter 10, "Captives," and ask for an oral or written narration.

Grades 10–12: Read together or assign as independent reading *Augustus Caesar's World*, pages 137–151, "The Druids" through "The Pantheon," and ask for an oral or written narration.

Tip: Make sure older children are up to date with their Discovering Doctrine *notebooks and their Book of Centuries entries.*

Reminder: Get The Roman Colosseum *for lesson 155 for Family. You will also need* Peril and Peace *for grades 10–12 in lesson 156 and for Family in lesson 160.*

Lesson 146: Paul's Farewell

Materials Needed
- Bible
- (optional) *The Stuff They Left Behind: From the Days of Ancient Rome*
- *Then and Now Bible Maps,* dry erase marker
- *Foundations in Romans* (grades 7–12)
- *The Apostle: A Life of Paul* (grades 10–12)

Family: Ask the students what they recall about Paul's third missionary journey so far and especially the riot in Ephesus.

If desired, display and discuss the picture of the statue of Diana of the Ephesians from *The Stuff They Left Behind: From the Days of Ancient Rome*. (See Parental Discretion note in portfolio.)

Read together Acts 20:2–38 and ask for an oral narration. Have the students continue tracing the stops on Paul's third missionary journey onto the map 14 overlay in *Then and Now Bible Maps* as you read about them.

Book of Centuries Timeline

Grades 7–12: Continue working on *Foundations in Romans*, lesson 14.

Grades 10–12: Read together or assign as independent reading *The Apostle: A Life of Paul*, chapters 27 and 28, "Affliction in Asia" and "A Treatise for Rome."

Lesson 147: Paul Arrested in Jerusalem

Materials Needed
- Bible
- *Then and Now Bible Maps,* dry erase marker
- *Foundations in Romans* (grades 7–12)
- *The Apostle: A Life of Paul* (grades 10–12)

Family: Ask the students what they remember from last time's reading about Paul's continued travels and his route to arrive in Jerusalem. Read together Acts 21:1–17 and have the students finish tracing the stops on Paul's third missionary journey onto the map 14 overlay in *Then and Now Bible Maps* as you read about them.

Explain that this trip to Jerusalem would prove to be one more step in God's plan to spread the gospel throughout the Roman Empire. Read together Acts 21:18—22:29 and ask for an oral narration.

Grades 7–12: Finish *Foundations in Romans*, lesson 14, this week.

Grades 10–12: Read together or assign as independent reading *The Apostle: A Life of Paul*, chapters 29 and 30, "Facing the Future" and "Riot in Jerusalem."

Lesson 148: Visit 30 to Europe & Various Readings

Materials Needed
- *Visits to Europe*
- *Galen and the Gateway to Medicine* (grades 4–6)
- *The Apostle: A Life of Paul* (grades 10–12)

Family: Complete Visit 30 in *Visits to Europe*.

Grades 4–6: Read together or assign as independent reading *Galen and the Gateway to Medicine*, the last half of chapter 4, "Galen Begins to Study Medicine," pages 31–36, and ask for an oral or written narration.

Grades 10–12: Read together or assign as independent reading *The Apostle: A Life of Paul*, chapters 31 and 32, "The Torture Chamber" and "King, Queen, and Governor."

TERM 3

Lesson 149: Paul on Trial

Materials Needed
- Bible
- *Augustus Caesar's World* OR *For the Temple* (grades 7–9)
- *Augustus Caesar's World* (grades 10–12)

Family: Ask the students what they remember from last time's reading about Paul's arrest. Read together Acts 22:30—24:27 and ask for an oral narration.

> *Tip:* Felix was the Rome-appointed governor of Judea during A.D. 52–58. He lost his position and Porcius Festus replaced him for A.D. 58–62.

Grades 7–9: Read together or assign as independent reading *Augustus Caesar's World*, pages 224–232, "Stepstons and Stars" and "Strabo and the World," OR *For the Temple*, chapter 11, "A Tale of Civil Strife," and ask for an oral or written narration.

Grades 10–12: Read together or assign as independent reading *Augustus Caesar's World*, pages 152–165, "A Bible for the Romans" through "Who Were the Roman Gods?," and ask for an oral or written narration.

Lesson 150: Paul Appeals to Caesar Nero

Materials Needed
- Bible
- *Galen and the Gateway to Medicine* (grades 4–6)
- *Augustus Caesar's World* OR *For the Temple* (grades 7–9)
- *Augustus Caesar's World* (grades 10–12)

Family: Ask the students what they remember from last time's reading about Paul's case. Read together Acts 25:1—26:32 and ask for an oral narration. Explain that Nero was Caesar at this time.

> *Tip:* Agrippa II, son of Herod Agrippa I (Acts 12:1), ruled the territories northeast of Palestine, because he was a friend of the Roman imperial family. He had extensive background and knowledge of the Jews' religion and would be helpful to Festus, the newcomer.

Grades 4–6: Read together or assign as independent reading *Galen and the Gateway to Medicine*, chapter 5, "About Hippocrates," and ask for an oral or written narration.

Grades 7–9: Read together or assign as independent reading *Augustus Caesar's World*, pages 233–238, "Of Calendars and the Mayans," OR *For*

Book of Centuries Timeline

TERM 3

Book of Centuries Timeline

the Temple, chapter 12, "Desultory Fighting," and ask for an oral or written narration.

Grades 10–12: Read together or assign as independent reading *Augustus Caesar's World*, pages 166–182, "Golden Eagles Come Home" through "Herod and the Temple," and ask for an oral or written narration.

Lesson 151: Paul in Rome

Materials Needed
- Bible
- *Then and Now Bible Maps*
- *Foundations in Romans* (grades 7–12)
- *The Apostle: A Life of Paul* (grades 10–12)

Family: Ask students what they recall from last time's reading about Paul's trial. Read together Acts 27:1—28:31 and ask for an oral narration.

Have the students follow Paul's journey to Rome on the map 14 overlay in *Then and Now Bible Maps*.

Tip: During this two-year imprisonment, Paul wrote the "Prison Epistles": Ephesians, Colossians, Philemon, and Philippians. He was then released for a short time but was taken prisoner and executed in Rome in A.D. 67.

Grades 7–12: Begin working on *Foundations in Romans*, lesson 15.

Grades 10–12: Read together or assign as independent reading *The Apostle: A Life of Paul*, chapters 33 and 34, "Shipwreck" and "Capital of the World."

Lesson 152: The Christians Persecuted

Materials Needed
- *The Story of the Romans*
- *Foundations in Romans* (grades 7–12)
- *The Apostle: A Life of Paul* (grades 10–12)

Family: Ask students what they recall from last time's reading about Paul's imprisonment under Caesar Nero. Explain that the Bible narrative ends there, but we can pick up the story of history from other accounts and find out what happened to the Christians and the Roman Empire. Read together *The Story of the Romans*, chapters 78 and 79, "The Christians Persecuted" and "Nero's Cruelty." Ask for an oral narration.

New Testament written as letters to first Christian churches in Roman Empire (52—96)

First persecution of Christians under Nero; Peter and Paul killed (64—68)

Judea revolts against Rome (66)

Grades 7–12: Continue working on *Foundations in Romans*, lesson 15.

Grades 10–12: Read together or assign as independent reading *The Apostle: A Life of Paul*, chapters 35 and 36, "The Years of Freedom" and "No Kind of Death."

Lesson 153: Visit 31 to Europe & Various Readings

Materials Needed
- *Visits to Europe*
- *Galen and the Gateway to Medicine* (grades 4–6)
- *The Apostle: A Life of Paul*, if needed (grades 10–12)

Family: Complete Visit 31 in *Visits to Europe*.

Grades 4–6: Read together or assign as independent reading *Galen and the Gateway to Medicine*, chapter 6, "Galen's Travels," and ask for an oral or written narration.

Grades 10–12: Use today to catch up on any reading in *The Apostle: A Life of Paul* as needed.

Lesson 154: Two Short Reigns

Materials Needed
- *The Story of the Romans*
- *The Stuff They Left Behind: From the Days of Ancient Rome*
- *Augustus Caesar's World* OR *For the Temple* (grades 7–9)
- *Augustus Caesar's World* (grades 10–12)

Family: Ask students what they recall from last time's reading about the end of Nero. Read together *The Story of the Romans*, chapters 80 and 81, "Two Short Reigns" and "The Siege of Jerusalem." Ask for an oral narration.

Display and discuss the picture of the Colosseum from *The Stuff They Left Behind: From the Days of Ancient Rome*.

Grades 7–9: Read together or assign as independent reading *Augustus Caesar's World*, pages 239–245, "Children of the Sun" and "Herod Is Dead," OR *For the Temple*, chapter 13, "The Test of Devotion," and ask for an oral or written narration.

Grades 10–12: Read together or assign as independent reading *Augustus Caesar's World*, pages 182–194, "Hillel, the Great Pharisee" through "Augustus, the God," and ask for an oral or written narration.

Book of Centuries Timeline

TERM 3

Book of Centuries Timeline

Lesson 155: The Roman Colosseum

Materials Needed
- *The Roman Colosseum*
- *Galen and the Gateway to Medicine* (grades 4–6)
- *Augustus Caesar's World* OR *For the Temple* (grades 7–9)
- *Augustus Caesar's World* (grades 10–12)

Family: Ask students what they recall from last time's reading about Vespasian, the emperor who built the Colosseum. Read together the first half of *The Roman Colosseum*.

Grades 4–6: Read together or assign as independent reading *Galen and the Gateway to Medicine*, chapter 7, "Alexandria!," and ask for an oral or written narration.

Grades 7–9: Read together or assign as independent reading *Augustus Caesar's World*, pages 246–257, "The Old Silk Road" and "Land of the Dragon," OR *For the Temple*, chapter 14, "Jerusalem," and ask for an oral or written narration.

Grades 10–12: Read together or assign as independent reading *Augustus Caesar's World*, pages 195–209, "A Roman Pharaoh" through "Remember Akhenaton," and ask for an oral or written narration.

Tip: Make sure older children are up to date with their Discovering Doctrine *notebooks and their Book of Centuries entries.*

Lesson 156: The Roman Colosseum (concluded)

Materials Needed
- *The Roman Colosseum*
- *Foundations in Romans* (grades 7–12)
- *Peril and Peace* (grades 10–12)

Family: Ask students what they recall from last time's reading about the Colosseum. Read together the last half of *The Roman Colosseum*.

Grades 7–12: Continue working on *Foundations in Romans*, lesson 15.

Grades 10–12: Read together or assign as independent reading *Peril and Peace*, pages 11–14, "What was the Ancient Church?"

Lesson 157: The Buried Cities

Materials Needed
- *The Story of the Romans*
- *The Stuff They Left Behind: From the Days of Ancient Rome*
- *Foundations in Romans* (grades 7–12)
- *Peril and Peace* (grades 10–12)

Family: Display and discuss the picture of the Arch of Titus from *The Stuff They Left Behind: From the Days of Ancient Rome*.
   Read together *The Story of the Romans*, chapters 82 and 83, "The Buried Cities" and "The Terrible Banquet." Ask for an oral narration.

Grades 7–12: Finish working on *Foundations in Romans*, lesson 15, this week.

Grades 10–12: Read together or assign as independent reading *Peril and Peace*, pages 15–24, "Paul: A Servant of the True God."

Lesson 158: Visit 32 to Europe & Various Readings

Materials Needed
- *Visits to Europe*
- *Hungry Planet: What the World Eats*
- *Galen and the Gateway to Medicine* (grades 4–6)
- *Peril and Peace* (grades 10–12)

Family: Complete Visit 32 in *Visits to Europe*.

Grades 4–6: Read together or assign as independent reading *Galen and the Gateway to Medicine*, chapter 8, "Galen and the Gladiators," and ask for an oral or written narration.

Grades 10–12: Read together or assign as independent reading *Peril and Peace*, pages 25–27, "Terrible Trials and Persecutions."

Lesson 159: The Emperor's Tablets

Materials Needed
- *The Story of the Romans*
- *The Stuff They Left Behind: From the Days of Ancient Rome*
- *Augustus Caesar's World* OR *For the Temple* (grades 7–9)
- *Augustus Caesar's World* (grades 10–12)

TERM 3

Book of Centuries Timeline

Titus destroys Jerusalem (70)

Pompeii and Herculaneum buried by eruption of Vesuvius; dedication of Roman Colosseum (79)

Book of Centuries Timeline

Apostle John banished to Patmos (96)

Roman Empire at its greatest extent under Trajan (98—117)

Polycarp, disciple of John, martyred (155)

Family: Ask students what they recall from last time's reading about the cities of Pompeii and Herculaneum. Display and discuss the picture of the Dyer Shop Fresco in Pompeii from *The Stuff They Left Behind: From the Days of Ancient Rome*.

Read together *The Story of the Romans*, chapters 84–86, "The Emperor's Tablets," "The Good Trajan," and "Trajan's Column." Ask for an oral narration.

Grades 7–9: Read together or assign as independent reading *Augustus Caesar's World*, pages 258–264, "Of India and the Hindus," OR *For the Temple*, chapter 15, "The Siege Is Begun," and ask for an oral or written narration.

Grades 10–12: Read together or assign as independent reading *Augustus Caesar's World*, pages 210–223, "Philo and the Lighthouse" through "Questions and Answers," and ask for an oral or written narration.

Lesson 160: Polycarp

Materials Needed
- *Peril and Peace*
- *Galen and the Gateway to Medicine* (grades 4–6)
- *Augustus Caesar's World* OR *For the Temple* (grades 7–9)
- *Augustus Caesar's World* (grades 10–12)

Family: Ask students what they recall about the emperor Trajan. Explain that you will be reading some stories about early Christians who lived and died during the time of the Roman emperors. Today you will read a story about Polycarp, who lived during the reign of Trajan. Read together *Peril and Peace*, pages 29–41, "Polycarp: Ground Like Wheat in the Lion's Teeth."

Grades 4–6: Read together or assign as independent reading *Galen and the Gateway to Medicine*, chapter 9, "Galen Goes to Rome," and ask for an oral or written narration.

Grades 7–9: Read together or assign as independent reading *Augustus Caesar's World*, pages 265–272, "Pater Patriae" and "Buddha and the Kingdom of Truth," OR *For the Temple*, chapter 16, "The Subterranean Passage," and ask for an oral or written narration.

Grades 10–12: Read together or assign as independent reading *Augustus Caesar's World*, pages 224–238, "Stepsons and Stars" through "Of Calendars and the Mayans," and ask for an oral or written narration.

Lesson 161: The Great Wall

Materials Needed
- *The Story of the Romans*

- *The Stuff They Left Behind: From the Days of Ancient Rome*
- *Foundations in Romans* (grades 7–12)

Family: Display and discuss the picture of Trajan's Column from *The Stuff They Left Behind: From the Days of Ancient Rome*.
  Read together *The Story of the Romans*, chapters 87–89, "The Great Wall," "Hadrian's Death," and "Antoninus Pius." Ask for an oral narration.

Grades 7–12: Begin working on *Foundations in Romans*, lesson 16.

Lesson 162: The Model Pagan

Materials Needed
- *The Story of the Romans*
- *Foundations in Romans* (grades 7–12)
- *Peril and Peace* (grades 10–12)

Family: Ask students what they recall from last time's reading about Hadrian, his wall, and his successor, good Antoninus. Read together *The Story of the Romans*, chapters 90 and 91, "The Model Pagan" and "Another Cruel Emperor." Ask for an oral narration.

Grades 7–12: Continue working on *Foundations in Romans*, lesson 16.

Grades 10–12: Read together or assign as independent reading *Peril and Peace*, pages 43–52, "Justin: A Flame Was Kindled in My Soul."

Lesson 163: Visit 33 to Europe & Various Readings

Materials Needed
- *Visits to Europe*
- *Galen and the Gateway to Medicine* (grades 4–6)
- *Peril and Peace* (grades 10–12)

Family: Complete Visit 33 in *Visits to Europe*.

Grades 4–6: Read together or assign as independent reading *Galen and the Gateway to Medicine*, the first half of chapter 10, "Dr. Galen's Medicine," pages 83–89, and ask for an oral or written narration.

Grades 10–12: Read together or assign as independent reading *Peril and Peace*, pages 53–56, "Worship in the Ancient Church."

Book of Centuries Timeline

Hadrian's Wall built across Britain (c. 117—138)

TERM 3

Book of Centuries Timeline

📖 Lesson 164: An Unnatural Son

Materials Needed
- *The Story of the Romans*
- *Augustus Caesar's World* OR *For the Temple* (grades 7–9)
- *Augustus Caesar's World* (grades 10–12)

Family: Ask students what they recall from last time's reading about Marcus Aurelius and the horrible plague that his co-ruler brought to the people. Read together *The Story of the Romans*, chapters 92–94, "An Unnatural Son," "The Senate of Women," and "The Gigantic Emperor." Ask for an oral narration.

Grades 7–9: Read together or assign as independent reading *Augustus Caesar's World*, pages 273–281, "December 25, Year 1," OR *For the Temple*, chapter 17, "The Capture of the Temple," and ask for an oral or written narration.

Grades 10–12: Read together or assign as independent reading *Augustus Caesar's World*, pages 239–249, "Children of the Sun" through "The Old Silk Road," and ask for an oral or written narration.

📖 Lesson 165: Origen

Materials Needed
- *Peril and Peace*
- *Galen and the Gateway to Medicine* (grades 4–6)
- *Augustus Caesar's World* OR *For the Temple* (grades 7–9)
- *Augustus Caesar's World* (grades 10–12)

Family: Ask students what they recall about the emperors Severus and Decius. Explain that the story today is about a Christian who lived under those two emperors' persecution. Read together *Peril and Peace,* pages 57–69, "Origen: God Planted in Us the Unspeakable Longing to Know."

Origen founds school in Alexandria (c. 200)

Grades 4–6: Read together or assign as independent reading *Galen and the Gateway to Medicine*, the last half of chapter 10, "Dr. Galen's Medicine," pages 90–95, and ask for an oral or written narration.

Grades 7–9: Read together or assign as independent reading *Augustus Caesar's World*, pages 282–286, "Tiberius" and "A Boy of Nazareth," OR *For the Temple*, chapter 18, "Slaves," and ask for an oral or written narration.

Grades 10–12: Read together or assign as independent reading *Augustus Caesar's World*, pages 250–264, "Land of the Dragon" through "Of India and the Hindus," and ask for an oral or written narration.

> **Tip:** Make sure older children are up to date with their *Discovering Doctrine* notebooks and their Book of Centuries entries.

Lesson 166: Invasion of the Goths

Materials Needed
- *The Story of the Romans*
- *Foundations in Romans* (grades 7–12)
- *Peril and Peace* (grades 10–12)

Family: Ask students what they recall about the one-thousandth anniversary that was celebrated during the reign of Philip. (He was the emperor whose general was Decius.) Explain that though Rome had existed and grown powerful over so many years, yet the end was coming. Read together *The Story of the Romans*, chapters 95 and 96, "Invasion of the Goths" and "Zenobia, Queen of Palmyra." Ask for an oral narration.

Grades 7–12: Continue working on *Foundations in Romans*, lesson 16.

Grades 10–12: Read together or assign as independent reading *Peril and Peace*, pages 71–86, "Cyprian: This Body Is My Sacrifice."

Lesson 167: A Prophecy Fulfilled

Materials Needed
- *The Story of the Romans*
- *Foundations in Romans* (grades 7–12)
- *Peril and Peace* (grades 10–12)

Family: Ask students what they recall about the invasion of the Goths and the queen of Palmyra. Discuss how no one wanted to be emperor of Rome because they feared violent deaths. Read together *The Story of the Romans*, chapters 97 and 98, "A Prophecy Fulfilled" and "The First Christian Emperor." Ask for an oral narration.

Grades 7–12: Finish working on *Foundations in Romans*, lesson 16, this week.

Grades 10–12: Read together or assign as independent reading *Peril and Peace*, pages 87–101, "Constantine: With This You Will Conquer."

Lesson 168: Visit 34 to Europe & Various Readings

Materials Needed
- *Visits to Europe*
- *Galen and the Gateway to Medicine* (grades 4–6)
- *Peril and Peace* (grades 10–12)

Book of Centuries Timeline

Romans defeated by the Ostrogoths; barbarian invasions on all sides (255)

Egypt taken by Zenobia, queen of Palmyra (269—273)

Diocletian divides the Roman Empire into western and eastern halves (285)

Emperor Constantine converts to Christianity (313)

TERM 3

Book of Centuries Timeline

Family: Complete Visit 34 in *Visits to Europe*.

Grades 4–6: Read together or assign as independent reading *Galen and the Gateway to Medicine*, chapter 11, "Galen's Pharmacy," and ask for an oral or written narration.

Grades 10–12: Read together or assign as independent reading *Peril and Peace*, pages 103 and 104, "Early Creeds and Councils."

Lesson 169: Athanasius

Materials Needed
- *Peril and Peace*
- *Augustus Caesar's World* OR *For the Temple* (grades 7–9)
- *Augustus Caesar's World* (grades 10–12)

Athanasius becomes bishop of Alexandria (328)

Family: Ask students what they recall about Constantine, the first Christian emperor. Explain that Athanasius was a Christian who lived during the reigns of Constantine and his sons. Read together *Peril and Peace*, pages 105–116, "Athanasius: Do Martyrs Die for a Mere Man?"

Grades 7–9: Read together or assign as independent reading *Augustus Caesar's World*, pages 287–297, "The Hebrew Prophets" and "On the German Border," OR *For the Temple*, chapter 19, "At Rome," and ask for an oral or written narration.

Grades 10–12: Read together or assign as independent reading *Augustus Caesar's World*, pages 265–272, "Pater Patriae" through "Buddha and the Kingdom of Truth," and ask for an oral or written narration.

Reminder: If you want to do a hands-on project for lesson 179 or 180, gather any supplies you might need.

Lesson 170: The Roman Empire Divided

Materials Needed
- *The Story of the Romans*
- *Galen and the Gateway to Medicine* (grades 4–6)
- *Augustus Caesar's World* OR *For the Temple* (grades 7–9)
- *Augustus Caesar's World* (grades 10–12)

Family: Ask students what they recall about Julian the Apostate. Read together *The Story of the Romans*, chapters 99 and 100, "The Roman Empire Divided" and "An Emperor's Penance." Ask for an oral narration.

Grades 4–6: Read together or assign as independent reading *Galen and the Gateway to Medicine*, chapter 12, "Galen Serves the Emperors," and ask for an oral or written narration.

Grades 7–9: Read together or assign as independent reading *Augustus Caesar's World*, pages 298–307, "The Passover" and "My Dear Tiberius," if reading this book, and ask for an oral or written narration. Or use today to catch up on any assigned reading in *For the Temple* if needed.

Grades 10–12: Read together or assign as independent reading *Augustus Caesar's World*, pages 273–286, "December 25, Year 1" through "A Boy of Nazareth," and ask for an oral or written narration.

Lesson 171: Ambrose

Materials Needed
- *Peril and Peace*
- *Foundations in Romans* (grades 7–12)

Family: Ask students what they recall about the emperor Theodosius and the one stain on his memory. Explain that today's story tells more about the church father who stood up to him: Ambrose. Read together *Peril and Peace*, pages 133–143, "Ambrose: A Bishop Cannot Give Up the Temple of the Lord."

Grades 7–12: Begin working on *Foundations in Romans*, lesson 17.

Grades 10–12: Read together or assign as independent reading *Peril and Peace*, pages 117–131, "The Great Cappadocians: Perhaps You Have Never Met a Bishop."

Lesson 172: Augustine

Materials Needed
- *Peril and Peace*
- *Foundations in Romans* (grades 7–12)

Family: Explain that at the same time Ambrose was leading a church in Italy, another man named Augustine was living in North Africa. He would eventually become one of the most well-known of all the church fathers. Read together *Peril and Peace,* pages 145–162, "Augustine: Our Hearts Are Restless Until They Rest in You."

Grades 7–12: Continue working on *Foundations in Romans*, lesson 17.

Grades 10–12: Read together or assign as independent reading *Peril and Peace*, pages 163–174, "John Chrysostom: Vanity of Vanities."

Book of Centuries Timeline

Ambrose defies Emperor Theodosius *(390)*

Augustine begins writing City of God *(413)*

TERM 3

Book of Centuries Timeline

Lesson 173: Visit 35 to Europe & Various Readings

Materials Needed
- *Visits to Europe*
- *Galen and the Gateway to Medicine* (grades 4–6)
- *Peril and Peace* (grades 10–12)

Family: Complete Visit 35 in *Visits to Europe*.

Grades 4–6: Read together or assign as independent reading *Galen and the Gateway to Medicine*, the first half of chapter 13, "After Galen," pages 110–116, and ask for an oral or written narration.

Grades 10–12: Read together or assign as independent reading *Peril and Peace*, pages 175–177, "How Did We Get the Bible?"

Lesson 174: Jerome

Materials Needed
- *Peril and Peace*
- *Augustus Caesar's World*, if needed (grades 7–9)
- *Augustus Caesar's World* (grades 10–12)

Family: Explain that today you will read the story of another church leader; this one, Jerome, lived near Israel. Read together *Peril and Peace*, pages 179–190, "Jerome: Love the Holy Scriptures, and Wisdom Will Love You."

Grades 7–9: Read together or assign as independent reading *Augustus Caesar's World*, pages 308–314, "Hermann, the German Hero" and "Farewell Augustus!," if reading this book, and ask for an oral or written narration.

Grades 10–12: Read together or assign as independent reading *Augustus Caesar's World*, pages 287–304, "The Hebrew Prophets" through "The Passover," and ask for an oral or written narration.

Jerome translates the Scriptures in Latin (The Vulgate) (404)

Lesson 175: Sieges of Rome

Materials Needed
- *The Story of the Romans*
- *Galen and the Gateway to Medicine* (grades 4–6)
- *Augustus Caesar's World*, if needed (grades 7–9)
- *Augustus Caesar's World* (grades 10–12)

Family: Ask students what they recall about the Goths and other barbarians who were invading Roman territory. Read together *The Story of the Romans*,

End of Western Roman Empire (476); Eastern Roman Empire continues at Constantinople until conquered by Turks in 1453

chapters 101 and 102, "Sieges of Rome" and "End of the Empire of the West." Ask for an oral narration.

Grades 4–6: Read together or assign as independent reading *Galen and the Gateway to Medicine*, the last half of chapter 13, "After Galen," pages 116–123, and ask for an oral or written narration.

Grades 7–9: Read together or assign as independent reading *Augustus Caesar's World*, pages 315–325, "The Kingdom of Heaven" and "A New Religion for Rome," if reading this book, and ask for an oral or written narration.

Grades 10–12: Read together or assign as independent reading *Augustus Caesar's World*, pages 305–325, "My Dear Tiberius" through "A New Religion for Rome," and ask for an oral or written narration.

Tip: Make sure older children are up to date with their Discovering Doctrine *notebooks and their Book of Centuries entries.*

Book of Centuries Timeline

Lesson 176: Bible Exam or Catch Up

Materials Needed
- Bible (if needed for catch-up reading)
- *Foundations in Romans* (grades 7–12)

Family: Use this day to catch up on any reading you need to finish, or use the questions below for the students' exam on the book of Acts.
Grades 1–3: Tell a story about Peter after Jesus ascended to Heaven.
Grades 4–6: Tell all you remember about the believers who were gathered in Jerusalem when they heard about and trusted in Jesus.
Grades 7–9: Tell in full how Saul was converted.
Grades 10–12: Tell all you can remember about the obstacles Paul encountered on his missionary journeys.

Grades 7–12: Continue working on *Foundations in Romans*, lesson 17.

Lesson 177: Bible Exam or Catch Up

Materials Needed
- Bible (if needed for catch-up reading)
- *Foundations in Romans* (grades 7–12)

Family: Use this day to catch up on any reading you need to finish, or use the questions below for the students' exam on the book of Acts.

Book of Centuries Timeline

Grades 1–3: Tell a story about Paul (Saul).
Grades 4–6: Tell a story from one of Paul's missionary journeys.
Grades 7–9: "What must I do to be saved?" Tell all you can remember about who said this to whom and the circumstances surrounding it.
Grades 10–12: Tell in full about Paul's arrest, trial, and imprisonment recorded in the final chapters of Acts. Add any details that you found interesting from your readings in *The Apostle*.

Grades 7–12: Finish *Foundations in Romans*, lesson 17.
   Select a chapter from Romans 12–16 and ask for a narration. Allow the student to look at the chapter outline in *Foundations in Romans* if necessary.

Lesson 178: Visit 36 to Europe

Materials Needed
- *Visits to Europe*
- (optional) *Peril and Peace* (grades 10–12)

Family: Complete Visit 36 in *Visits to Europe*.

Optional Grades 10–12: Read together or assign as independent reading *Peril and Peace*, pages 191–203, "Patrick: Come Walk among Us."

Tip: Patrick will also be included in the Middle Ages, Renaissance, Reformation & Epistles study. You may assign this reading to introduce him or choose to omit this reading and wait for that study.

Lesson 179: Ancient Rome Catch Up, Project, or Exam

Materials Needed
- (optional) Materials for hands-on project
- (optional) *Peril and Peace* (grades 10–12)

Family: Use this day to catch up on any reading you need to finish, or use the questions below for the students' exam on their Ancient Rome readings. You may also use this lesson and the next to do an optional hands-on project.
Grades 1–3: Tell about one of Rome's emperors of whom you read this term.
Grades 4–6: Describe in detail either a Roman city or the Colosseum and what it was used for.
Grades 7–9: Tell all you know about the emperor to whom the Apostle Paul appealed.
Grades 10–12: Select three church fathers of whom you read this term and

tell their stories. What struggles did the early church face, both from within and without?

Optional Grades 10–12: Read together or assign as independent reading *Peril and Peace*, pages 205–217, "Benedict: Renounce Yourself and Follow Christ."

Tip: Benedict is also included in the Middle Ages, Renaissance, Reformation & Epistles study.

Optional Hands-On Project: Select a hands-on project from the Links and Tips page at http://simplycm.com/matthew-links.

Lesson 180: Ancient Rome Catch Up, Project, or Exam

Materials Needed
- (optional) Materials for hands-on project

Family: Use this day to catch up on any reading you need to finish, or use the questions below for the students' exam on their Ancient Rome readings. You may also do an optional hands-on project.
Grades 1–3: Tell about one of the early church fathers of whom you read this term.
Grades 4–6: Tell all you can remember about Constantine.
Grades 7–9: "God, you have made us for yourself and our hearts are restless until they rest in you." Who does this statement describe? Tell about his restlessness and how he eventually found rest in God.
Grades 10–12: Explain how the Roman Empire grew and how it fell, relating both the events and the causes of each.

Optional Hands-On Project: Continue your selected hands-on project or start a new one if desired.

Book of Centuries Timeline

Helpful Information

Why I Wrote These Lessons

When I was growing up in Sunday School and church, I heard the stories of the Bible many times. I could tell you all the details of Who, What, Why, and How. But I never thought about the When. I knew those Bible accounts were true, just like the history accounts I read were true, but I never put the two subjects together to comprehend how Bible events fit into world history events.

I also never thought about how the different Bible stories fit together. For example, I knew the story of Joseph's being sold into slavery and eventually rising into the place of leadership in Egypt, and I knew the story of Moses and the Exodus, but I never connected the two mentally as a sort of cause and effect until I studied them with my children in chronological order. Suddenly all the pieces started fitting together!

After that experience, I knew how I wanted to teach my children the Bible: in chronological order alongside world history—and I wanted to make the Bible history most important. Charlotte Mason emphasized the priority Bible lessons should have in our curriculum: "Their Bible lessons should help them to realise in early days that the knowledge of God is the principal knowledge, and, therefore, that their Bible lessons are their chief lessons" (Vol. 1, p. 251). As our children study Bible accounts intertwined with world history, they learn to see God's hand of sovereignty moving in the events. They come to know God's character through His Word and begin to interpret world happenings through a Biblical worldview. They absorb God's truth and can discern and refute false beliefs that man has embraced throughout history.

So the lessons in this book will walk you through Scripture passages to read, living books to use, and optional hands-on activities to do as you continue working your way through the Bible—from Matthew through Acts, including Ancient Rome. You'll also find narration ideas, teaching tips, and Book of Centuries dates to help you see how the Bible accounts fit into world history events.

One of my main goals is to show you how you can teach the same historical time period to all of your children at the same time, no matter what grades they are in. I firmly believe in the advantages that a one-room schoolhouse approach can bring. You will save time in both planning and teaching, and your children will grow together in community as they learn together and help each other.

Please keep in mind that this study is just a collection of suggestions. I'm simply passing along these suggestions to, hopefully, save you some time and give you some ideas. You know your children much better than I do, so feel free to change, add, or omit as you see fit. Remember, I used the books that were available to me; they may not be available to you. Don't be afraid to substitute.

Most of all, encourage the older children to help the younger, and allow the younger to look over the shoulder of the older; and together, enjoy these family studies of God's Word and history.

Charlotte Mason Methods Used in This Study

Living Books

Probably the most well known of Charlotte Mason's methods is her use of living books instead of dry, factual textbooks. Living books are usually written by one person who has a passion for the subject and writes in conversational or narrative style. The books pull you into the subject and involve your emotions, so it's easy to remember the events and facts. Living books make the subject "come alive." The books used in this study are living books. If you make a substitution, please do your best to select a living book.

Bible Readings: The Bible is the best living book! And Charlotte encouraged us to give our children plenty of direct contact with the Bible itself, not feed them just watered down retellings. So you will find throughout the lessons, the Scripture passages to read aloud directly from the Bible.

Narration

When you ask a child to narrate, you're asking him to tell back in his own words what he just saw, heard, or read. The narration can be oral or written or drawn—whatever. Because the child must think through the information and determine how to present it, mixed with his own opinion and impressions, this method of evaluation requires a much higher thinking level than mere fill-in-the-blank or answer-the-posed-question-with-a-fact methods. When requesting a child to narrate, word the question in an open, essay-type form, such as "Tell all you know about ___" or "Describe ___."

Oral Narration with Many Children: Usually it's good to start with the youngest child, then work your way up the ages asking if each has anything to add. However, if you use this approach every single time, the older ones might get complacent. ("No, nothing to add.") So you can mix things up a little by calling on any child at random to start the narration sometimes. Not knowing who will be selected to give the oral narration keeps everybody alert and listening. The key is to have one child start the narration and then have the others add to it, not repeat it. That mental exercise of remembering what was already mentioned and searching through your mind for something new to talk about is also a plus!

Written Narration: Older children can be expected to take the next step and write their narrations. If your older child is not used to doing narration, give him several weeks or months to get used to the idea and have some practice narrating orally first. It's harder to keep your train of thought when you have to also think about the mechanics of writing, punctuating, capitalizing, and all such trappings, so make sure your child is adept and successful with organizing and expressing his thoughts orally before adding the writing aspect. Once he is an "old pro" at oral narrations, you can ease him into the written narrations by requiring just one a week or so to begin with. The lessons in this book will give suggestions for some written narrations. You can determine which of your students can handle those assignments.

Also keep in mind that you can do narration in many ways. Oral is the quickest and simplest. But if you would like to keep things fresh, you can have the children express what they learned in various ways. We have a list of narration ideas on our website that might help you: http://simplycm.com/narration-ideas.

Book of Centuries

A Book of Centuries is like a timeline in a notebook. As its name suggests, each two-page spread in the book is devoted to one hundred years—a century—of history. Each student creates his or her own book, recording historical events and names of importance, along with pictures, poems, quotes, and anything else that makes the book individual. You can also add written narrations, illustrations from the Internet, or titles of books you've read that are set in that time period. As they add more history to the book, the students begin to make relations between people who lived in the same era.

Books of Centuries can be as simple or elaborate as you desire. If you want a simple one, download a free Book of Centuries template at http://simplycm.com/BOC.

We recommend each student in grades 7–12 create his own Book of Centuries. If your students are not yet old enough to take on the responsibility of their own Books of Centuries, you could create one together as a family.

Watch for helpful dates in the timeline column throughout the lessons in this book. You don't have to add every event listed; feel free to pick and choose. Dates are taken from *All Through the Ages,* revised second edition. If you are using a reference book that presents alternate dates, feel free to use those instead in your Book of Centuries. The purpose of this book is not to defend or refute certain dating, but to try to place Bible events in the broad context of world events. (Note: A "c" beside a date stands for "circa," which means "about" or "approximately.")

A Word on Mythology

When studying Ancient History, you will inevitably encounter mythology. Be careful about allowing young children to fill their minds with stories about false gods and goddesses. They need to know that these people who lived in ancient times worshiped false gods and invented stories about them, but they do not need to spend large amounts of time studying those false gods and learning every detail about those stories. Instead, make sure your children have a firm foundation in the truth about the one true God and interpret mythology through what Scripture says about it.

We often refer to Romans 1:20–25 when studying mythology. God's power, attributes (characteristics), and divine nature (the fact that He is the one true God) are clearly seen in His creation. The ancients saw His handiwork but they chose not to honor Him or give Him thanks. Instead, they chose to turn their worship to gods in the form of men and beasts (v. 23). They exchanged the truth of God for a lie and worshiped and served things that He created rather than the Creator Himself (v. 25).

Usually, I explain mythology something like this: "Myths are pretend stories these people made up instead of believing in God. Reading them can give us a good peek inside these people's hearts, because they often imagined their gods to be the same way they were themselves (moody, revengeful, selfish, etc.). Just keep in mind that the stories are pretend."

If you are following the Simply Charlotte Mason Curriculum Guide's suggestions for History and Bible, your child will have a good foundation in Scripture and truth before he is exposed to Greek and Roman mythology. Older children can learn more about mythology details than younger children, but still beware of how much mythology they are filling their minds with. I try to make sure that the children are getting as much (or more!) Bible into their minds as they are getting myths inside them during these Ancient History studies.

Suggestions toward Calculating Credits

Keeping track of high school credits is always a challenge but not that hard once you get the hang of it. You can calculate the credits based on actual time spent interacting with the material, or you can calculate credits based on the amount of work involved. Most authorities agree that if you are calculating based on actual time spent, a credit is awarded for every 120–180 hours spent on task, with 150 being average.

For the completion of grades 7–9 or 10–12 assignments in this Matthew through Acts & Ancient Rome study, I suggest that students should be awarded ½ credit for History/Geography, plus ½ credit for Bible. Usually Geography is included with History and considered one course of study. It is up to you whether you want to consider Bible as a separate course or include it as part of History, since the focus is on Israel's history in ancient times. If you want to combine History, Geography, and Bible, award 180 hours, or 1 full History credit.

Below are details demonstrating how the credit suggestions for this study were calculated. The calculations for Hours Spent are an estimated average. The calculations below for the Course Work Detail assume the student completed all the readings and assignments given in these lesson plans for grades 7–9 or 10–12.

Hours Spent

History & Geography—½ Credit
Average 2.5 hours per week x 36 weeks = 90 hours

Bible—½ Credit
Average 2.5 hours per week x 36 weeks = 90 hours

Course Work Detail

History

Grades 7–9
1007 pages read in 6 books
44 written narrations
16 artifacts studied
Book of Centuries project
3 essay exams

Grades 10–12
1566 pages read in 7 books
43 written narrations
16 artifacts studied
Book of Centuries project
3 essay exams

Geography

Grades 7–12
25 map studies and drills
126 pages read in 2 books
24 integrated map work in History and Bible lessons

Bible

Grades 7–12
158 pages read in 1 book (grades 7–9)
456 pages read in 2 books (grades 10–12)
190-page Bible study of Romans
Discovering Doctrine project
3 essay exams